The Life of
My Years

The Life of My Years

Prince A. Taylor, Jr.

Abingdon Press
Nashville

The Life of My Years

Copyright © 1983 by Abingdon Press

Library of Congress Cataloging in Publication Data

TAYLOR, PRINCE ALBERT, 1907–
  The life of my years.
  Bibliography: p.
  1. Taylor, Prince Albert, 1907–
  2. Methodist Church—United States—Bishops—Biography.
  3. Afro-American Methodists—Biography. I. Title.
  BX8495.T26A34   1983   287'.6'0924 [B]   83-2725

ISBN 0-687-21854-3

***calligraphy, photography and book design
by J. S. Laughbaum***

MANUFACTURED BY THE PARTHENON PRESS AT
NASHVILLE, TENNESSEE, UNITED STATES OF AMERICA

*Dedicated
To my wife,
Annie Belle*

Preface

The vantage point from which I have attempted to write is that the true church of Christ is an inclusive community—a goal which the church must forever have before it. In this endeavor, the church has had its tragic and triumphant hours. The issue of race can be, and has been at times, a barrier or a benefaction—a source of separatism and conflict, or a catalyst for the enrichment of spiritual life. Whatever have been the benefits of separatism, in essence, it has fragmented the body and impaired its health.

Progress has traveled a slow and difficult path, making detours here and there. But despite the struggle, tremendous strides have been made in the last fifty years. I have lived as an ordained clergyman through these years, and have attempted to tell the story in autobiographical form since I have been involved in many aspects of its work.

I have felt the need to put my own life in a historical setting, depicting directly and indirectly some of the influences that shaped my life and led to my personal understanding of the meaning of the church and its demands of those who serve it.

I have not been seriously concerned with chronology, but with relationships and patterns—how the story holds together and what it means. *The Life of My Years* is an effort to put into words what life has been as I have observed and experienced it.

Acknowledgments

The persons to whom I am indebted are too numerous to mention by name. Among them are many friends who helped to make the story, as well as those who encouraged me to write it. To all of them I am profoundly grateful.

I am particularly indebted to the following persons: Dr. Albert Outler, Perkins School of Theology, who first suggested to me that I should write the story; Dr. James McCord, president of Princeton Theological Seminary, who invited me to be a visiting Fellow at the seminary for two years, which gave me access to its resources, and encouraged me to write the book; Mrs. Doris Parker; Isabella and Julius Jenkins (my daughter and son-in-law), who read the manuscript and gave helpful suggestions; and Mrs. Edna Atwood, who spent endless hours of typing and helped to give the book its shape.

Finally, to my wife, Annie Belle, without whose sharing of life the story could not have emerged. Her constant encouragement and critical suggestions have been invaluable.

Contents

I

The Early Years

"It was the coldest night I have ever experienced," my father used to say, referring to January 27, 1907, the night I was born in Hennessey, Oklahoma. In those days most babies were born in the home, and one was fortunate to secure the services of a doctor. There was no telephone in the house, and my father had to walk quite a distance to the home of the doctor. I am confident that both my father and the doctor would have been happier had I postponed my arrival until the light of day. I guess I had worked up a bit of impatience, after waiting nine months to see what the world is like.

My father, Prince Albert Taylor, Sr., and my mother, Bertha Ann Littles Taylor, were born just 21 miles from each other, and that is where they grew to adulthood. It was a long distance when one considers the mode of travel of that day—foot, horseback, buggy, or carriage. I never heard them discuss their romance, so I do not know how they met, nor how many times they saw each other before they were married.

My father was a Methodist preacher and began his work in the Mississippi Annual Conference (black), which it was called at that time. In his early ministry, he transferred to the old Lincoln Conference, which included the Oklahoma territory. He was of an adventurous nature, and no doubt was influenced by reports of virgin opportunities in this far-flung "promised land."

My father was 5 feet 11 inches tall and weighed 250 pounds. In his younger years he was a giant of strength—a hearty eater, who could always eat a little more. Strangely enough he had excellent health until he was around seventy, and lived until he was 84.

His eating habits remind me of the old man who was asked to tell the story of his long life. He said, "Alcohol and tobacco. I have been smoking since I was a child, and I drink everything I can get my hands on." My father never smoked or drank, but nothing he ate in quantity or quality ever seemed to bother him.

He was of a jolly disposition, and enjoyed mingling with people. He made friends easily, but was capable of losing them, too. One reason was because, along with his good nature, he seldom passed up an opportunity to be witty, even if it had the potential of offending people.

I remember one Sunday morning, for example, when he was talking to a group of church school teachers about being competent. These people had barely a rudimentary education, but they were some of the best trained in the little church. In emphasizing the need for training my father said, "It takes brains to teach a Sunday school. Some of us are like frogs—we have more mouth than brains."

One old saint said, "From here on out, we are going to let the brains have it." And they did. From then on, my older sisters had to teach the classes.

His mind was exceptionally keen, and would engage almost anybody in a discussion on historical events. Once when he was visiting the home of one of my sisters, a member of the church came to their home. My father began immediately to rattle off historical knowledge to him. The man seemed to have been listening intently. My father turned and asked, "Brother Jones, what is your profession?"

"I ain't got nawhn," he answered.

My father had tremendous physical strength. I once saw him put a bushel of peaches on his shoulder and carry it for five miles, and did not appear even weary at the end of the journey. He was fifty-three years old.

In those days preaching, especially among blacks, carried a highly dramatic and emotional tone, with a completely literal and sensational interpretation of the Scriptures. The minister could make hell so visible that when he preached, one had to struggle to keep from falling into it. My father deplored that approach. He was more of a teacher, and his preaching seldom stirred the emotions of people. He did not have the musical tone in his voice which aroused congregational enthusiasm and response. While he was recognized as a knowledgeable man, he was not one of the popular preachers. He sought to provoke thinking in a period when most people simply wanted to feel. Some would refer to religion as being "better felt than told." He would frequently say to his congregation, "Well now, hollering isn't preaching," but the average congregation in those days was not convinced.

The impression should not be carried, however, that every preacher with a musical voice was void of substance, nor that all the preachers who were lacking in voice compensated with content. Some of the men who had voices that could move congregations were outstanding preachers and effective leaders.

The black preacher was more than the pastor of a church or churches. He was usually the community leader—counselor on secular as well as religious matters, and frequently teacher of the community school. My father served in all these capacities, and was highly influential in many ways. He firmly believed that education was the solution to the problems of the black people, and encouraged it at every opportunity.

He was fearless in all his relationships, whether he was dealing with whites or blacks, in Mississippi or in Maine. Even those who were turned off by him at times, recognized him as a force to be dealt with, and held him in respect.

When he was pastor in Montrose, Mississippi, a rural

community, a man went to another man's home, killed him with a shotgun and fled. My father spotted the murderer hiding behind the church that night. He got his shotgun, eased around the building, brought the guilty man to bay, and held him until the sheriff arrived. He thought nothing of it except that he had done his duty as a good citizen, by not allowing a man who had committed murder to escape.

At one time, he had two churches, one at Hickory, and the other one at Newton, eight miles apart. We lived at Hickory and he preached at Newton every other Sunday, morning and evening. Because the last train had run before the service was over in the evening, he would walk those eight miles to be home, where he could superintend the school the next morning. The shortest route was down the railroad track. I have heard him tell stories about wildcats and other dangerous animals that would cross those tracks as he walked along.

My father was a peculiar combination. He was fearless, had an excellent mind, was highly skilled with his hands, a hard worker, was deeply devoted to his family, compassionate, and loyal to a fault to his friends (who often used and betrayed him). On the other hand, he was impulsive, impatient, intolerant, and at times inflexible. He was a builder, and had a lot of imagination; but he was too impatient to thoroughly complete a job or do it especially well.

The only time I remember getting fired was when I was working as his helper on a small building he was employed to erect. The man fired him and let me go along with him. It didn't seem to upset him, but I was a bit embarrassed.

My father had a legal mind, and knew the *Discipline* of the church as only a few people knew it. He enjoyed calling the hand of the bishop on legal technicalities in the sessions of the annual conferences. There were times when the bishop penalized him for it, but that made no difference; he would do it the next time just the same.

He and my mother supplemented each other in a

wonderful way, for in some of his weakest areas were her greatest strengths. She was a mild-mannered woman, about five feet six inches tall, and weighed ninety-six pounds. But she was a woman of great courage and determination, and a remarkable mother, whose dreams for her children never faltered nor faded. She was long-suffering, patient, sacrificial, had unending endurance, could mend breached relationships, which my father created in the congregations, and kept the children encouraged in their educational ventures when frequent moves from town to town interrupted their school programs. My father espoused education for the children, but it was my mother who saw to it that the dreams had opportunities for fulfillment. She did not allow my father to give up on our education when crises arose. She would always find a way out, and insist on that way being followed. She could supply the nudging that my father needed at those crucial moments to keep us going. My father was never willing to give up the dreams for the children, but there were times when he was ready to postpone them. Mother would always say no. Her skills of management were far superior to those of my father. She was greatly loved in every congregation my father ever served, even by those who at times became disenchanted with him.

She was the mother of fourteen children, all born within a period of twenty years. I was the fifth child and the first boy. My brother, Fenelon, just fourteen months younger than I, died in infancy. Along with the rearing of thirteen children, and all the household duties this entailed, my mother was active in the work of the church. She was a woman of great faith, and sought to live it every day.

I never knew a time when my mother was not physically frail, but her indomitable will and hidden resources of strength kept her constantly on the move. She lived to the age of sixty-nine, and died of cancer.

Soon after my birth, my father was appointed to a church in Guthrie, Oklahoma. A story that has become legend in our family is an incident that occurred in our moving from

Hennessey to Guthrie. We went by train and were met by a member of the church, who took us to the parsonage in his mule-drawn wagon. The distance was five miles. When we arrived and my mother began checking the children—calling the roll, so to speak—she discovered that my sister, Virgia, was missing. My father did not wait for anyone to take him, but ran back on foot to the little railroad station in search of the child. She was there. The ticket agent had taken her into his office, spread a blanket over her, and she was sound asleep. What a time of rejoicing!

My father was restless, and the land did not "flow with milk and honey," so when I was two years old, our family decided to move back to Mississippi. There were only five children at that time. Had there been all fourteen of us then, I doubt that my parents would have decided to move back.

Plans were made for our return, but we were delayed a day in leaving. The train on which we were to leave was wrecked, and many people were killed. My father always argued that our delay was due to special Providence. He had difficulty explaining to me why Providence allowed the others to make the trip and be killed.

II

The Shaping Years

My father's father was a slave until he was 16 years old. Ironically enough, he was the slave of a Methodist preacher in Noxubee County, Mississippi. It was rumored that my grandfather was really his master's son. I never heard him mention his father, but he frequently referred to "my old master" with deep affection. Having heard from word of mouth the wretched stories of slavery, and living in a period not long after its abolition, we, his grandchildren, did not warm up to this kindly reference.

My father's mother was born a slave also. She, too, remained a slave until she was 16.

The story that has been passed down through the family is that my father's great-grandmother was the daughter of an African chief in Nigeria, West Africa. She and other members of her tribe were lured onto a slave trader's vessel. The crew gave a dance and presented gifts to the Africans. Before they realized it, the ship was off to sea.

(This was in 1789, the year George Washington was elected president, and five years after the Methodist Episcopal Church was organized in America.)

The ship, with its unhappy human cargo, landed in Virginia, where they were sold as slaves. A lady named Miss Lucy Granger bought my father's great-grandmother. She gave birth to a daughter whose father was a white man. This daughter married a man who was a slave of Miss Granger's nephew, Tom Preston. To this couple were born four sons and five daughters, one of whom was my father's mother, born in 1849.

Miss Granger never married. She wanted her slaves to become free at her death, but her nephew, Tom Preston, persuaded her to let him have them, and at his death, he would set them free and send them to Liberia. Accordingly they were willed to Tom Preston for his lifetime. He was to teach them to read and write, and they were to be freed at his death. His will provided for my great-grandmother, her sons and daughters, and their children to be set free. Several thousand dollars from the Lucy Granger estate were to be used for their transportation to Liberia. My grandmother Annie and her brother George were to have gone as teachers. Their training, as one would expect, was exceedingly meager, and most of what they learned was by their own efforts.

These plans were all aborted. At the time of Tom Preston's death in Mississippi, that state had passed laws against the freeing of slaves, making the will null and void.

At this point there is a gap in the record. Nothing is known about the ten years following the death of Tom Preston. Whether or not the family fell into evil hands, I do not know.

I do remember hearing my grandmother talk about the courage of her father in not allowing the master to whip his children. The task of whipping a slave was usually a corporate act. No one person tried to do it alone, particularly if the slave resisted the lashing. My grandmother told me that once one of her brothers had displeased the master, so he and several others gathered to whip him. The method used was to put the slave across a log and give him an undetermined number of lashes. My great-grandfather insisted on the right to discipline his own children. When the boy was put across the log and given the first lash, his father protested. "Stop! Don't hit another lick." They left the boy alone, but decided they should discipline his father instead. They put him across the log and struck him once. He leaped from the log and repeated, "Stop! Don't hit another lick."

He survived the incident, and from that time on he seemed to have their respect. There never was another attempt to hit him or his family.

My grandmother and all of her family had learned to read and write. During the Civil War, her mother read the newspapers and kept up with the way the war was going, although the slave owners did not know it. She was a secret informer on the state of the war for the other slaves who could not read or write. This was at times risky, for there were slaves who could be used by their masters to find out what was being said and done among the slaves. Such slaves were usually known or suspected. When one of them was near where such secret conversations were being held, someone would say, "Shy bry standn" (a shy briar is standing), and the conversation would be diverted in another direction. Informers were considered troublemakers and were disciplined in many ways.

Two of my grandmother's brothers, Winston and George, ran away during the Civil War and joined the Union army. George was in the Clinton riots in Mississippi during the reconstruction period.

Five years after Emancipation, when my grandmother was twenty-one years old, she became one of the first black persons to receive what was known as a first-grade license to teach school. One became a teacher by passing an examination. The following licenses were issued: first grade, second grade, and third grade. The third grade license was obtainable by almost anyone who applied, since there was not a lot of exhibited concern, by those with the power to implement changes, regarding who taught the black children.

In 1870, my grandmother was sent by the state superintendent of education to Noxubee county to teach school. My grandfather, Cornelius Taylor, was one of her students. It is interesting to note that Cornelius, a young man of unusual intellectual ability, and a slave, if not a son, of a Methodist preacher, could not read or write. Of course, to teach the slaves to read and write in Mississippi was forbidden by law. It was not likely, therefore, that the master would have been inclined to teach the slaves. The southern preacher was one of the main guardians of societal patterns and would have been the last to break the rules. In fact, during the last fifteen years before the Civil War, many of the southern preachers were ardent defenders of slavery.

My grandfather was evidently as much a charmer as he was a student, for he and my grandmother married in 1874. The newlyweds moved to Rankin county, my grandmother's home, and bought a 360 acre farm. Land was cheap, about fifty cents an acre, and could be paid for on time. My grandmother was a woman of rare ingenuity and drive. She furnished the leadership which kept my grandfather on the move. They raised some of everything—cattle, hogs, turkeys, geese, chickens, honeybees. The crops were of a wide variety, including rice. Fruit and pecan trees were in abundance.

My mother's mother, Julia Eubanks (part Creek Indian), was born in Alabama, but her family migrated with the family who owned them to Smith county, Mississippi. My mother's father was born in Smith county, where he spent his entire life.

I was not around my maternal grandparents much and do not remember any conversations about their early life. I do recall that they owned a 260 acre farm, and my grandfather was a successful farmer. He was a lay preacher in the (then) Methodist Episcopal Church. My grandmother, Julia, died in her early 60s. My grandfather married again when he was around 65, and reared another family. He died at the ripe old age of 101.

III

School in Mississippi

As a child I spent many happy days on the farm with my grandparents. My father's churches were never too far away from the farm, and the children were frequent visitors. I was the oldest grandson, and it was my grandfather's ambition to send me to Tuskegee, where I could be trained as an agriculturist and take over the farm.

I had read Booker T. Washington's autobiography, and was greatly impressed that a man of such unsophisticated beginnings could found Tuskegee Institute. Dr. W. E. B. DuBois, one of Mr. Washington's greatest critics, characterized him as "the most distinguished southerner since Jefferson Davis. . . . He stands as the one recognized spokesman of his ten million fellows, and one of the most notable figures of seventy million . . ."

It was not my privilege to have gone to Tuskegee, however. My grandfather lost his health before I was old enough to go. The farm was not doing well, and although I enjoyed farm life, I was not drawn toward it as a life vocation.

When I was eleven years old, during the illness of my grandfather, my grandmother and I took charge of the farm. With hired help, we cultivated and harvested the crops. I learned to plow at that age, and worked regularly doing so the entire season.

The public schools for black children in Mississippi, when I was a boy, were horrible. If one could barely read and write, he or she could teach school. I remember hearing a teacher rebuke a student for saying "dis" instead of this. "Boy," she said, "don't say dis; dat's flat."

Of course, poor teachers usually begot poor students. Those were the days of the primer with its famous story about the dog Rover. The story began, "I see Rover. Rover is a dog . . ." As I recall it was among the first stories in the book. The teacher would take the student over it, again and again, until he could read it without aid. Sometimes it took several days. It happened that I "saw" Rover the first day, and the continued repetition drove me into complete frustration. One day I threw a piece of crayon that landed against the head of the student who was trying to read. The teacher whipped me, but at least it broke the monotony.

Our parents took special interest in our school work, and supplemented much that we missed during the day at school.

The North Carolinians used to chide us Mississippians by saying, "When folks here in North Carolina go crazy, they send them to Mississippi to teach school."

Of course, the black teachers were not the sole possessors of incompetence. There is an interesting story about a school superintendent—no doubt apocryphal, but descriptive nevertheless—who was making a routine visit to one of the black schools. He entered the school and took his seat in the rear of the room to observe the teacher teach and the students recite. It was customary for the teacher to call each student to stand up in front of the class and answer questions on the lesson for the day. It was Johnny's time to recite. "John, who wrote the Declaration of Independence?" the teacher asked. He fumbled a moment, and then said, "I don' know, I didn't." The disgusted teacher said, "Sit down boy." He returned to his seat. After a brief pause, the superintendent said, "Wait a minute. Call him back up there. I don't like his manners. I believe he did do it."

One really had to be there in those days to know what it was like. I remember attending elementary school in Jackson, Mississippi, where the white and black children fought every morning en route to segregated schools, and every evening on the way home. These were dangerous occasions. The white children had all sorts of myths concerning the black children, especially the boys. There were such myths as: the blacks were as physically strong as oxen, and were possessed with animalistic drives. The crowds of white children would not touch the blacks if the blacks were in crowds; but if a white group met one or two blacks, there was real trouble. The whites at times were armed with knives and rifles. One black could chase a half dozen whites, so when the whites made their attacks they were in gangs. I fought with them, not with hatred, but for my survival.

I remember more about Jackson, however, than the conflict with these children. One of the best teachers I have ever known was there—Miss Mary Jones. I understand that her formal education ended with the eighth grade. She would get an extremely low rating today on methods of teaching, and probably human relations, for she would not hesitate to throw a book across the classroom at the head of some student who was inattentive or disorderly. My sister, Helen, says Miss Jones kept her so frightened that she did not learn anything from her. Not so with me. She could make mathematics and grammar come alive for me as no one has ever done—before nor since. Despite all of her questionable methods and disposition, I still regard her as one of my greatest benefactors in the field of education.

Teaching such as hers proves wrong the assumption that all teachers of these little schools were inadequate. Some of them were amazing, although their formal training was limited. They were dedicated and often brilliant people, and gave to the students all they had. Many of them were thorough in what they knew, and in their own way communicated it skillfully. Some of their students went on through high school, college, and graduate school, and became distinguished leaders and scholars. These teachers taught not only subject matter, but also they inspired hope in their students and communicated to them a sense of worth and dignity. The little one-room school had its multiplicity of handicaps, but when it was in the hands of a master craftsman, much good frequently came out of it.

The greatest weakness was not the little one-room school, it was the indifference of the state of Mississippi to the education of black children. This predicament was expressed in 1871 by the bishops of the Methodist Episcopal Church in an appeal to pastors and members for help. "The time may come," they said, "when the states in the South will make some provision for the education of colored children now growing up in utter ignorance in their midst. But thus far, they have made none, nor perhaps can it soon be expected of them. Christian philanthropy must supply this lack."

Fifty years later there was no outstanding change in the interest of the South in the education of black children.

The gap was filled in a remarkable way by the Methodist Episcopal Church through the agency known as the Freedmen's Aid Society, and later as the Board of Education for Negroes. Many elementary schools throughout the South were organized. Some schools taught the students from kindergarten through college. Teachers from the North (white) with the missionary spirit came South and served with black teachers, a number of whom had equal competence and commitment.

It would be a mistake to presume that every northern teacher who went South was competent and committed. One has only to read Dr. Henry L. Swint's book, *The Northern Teacher in the South* to get examples of many with varying motives and efectiveness. Be this as it may, the blacks owe a great debt of gratitude to those teachers who were devoted and genuinely concerned about the welfare of black people.

There were other churches with large black memberships, such as Presbyterians, Baptists, and Congregational, who sought to help blacks in the educational process. It was my privilege and that of other members of my family to have attended some of these schools.

Just outside of Jackson is Tougaloo College, sponsored by

the Congregational Church. It offered opportunities to students who wanted to go to school, but did not have the money to do it. A student could work during the day the first year and take classes at night. By so doing, he or she could earn money to pay expenses the following year for day attendance, with some additional work after school. I took advantage of this opportunity when I was in the eighth and ninth grades.

It was at Haven Teachers College, earlier known as Meridian Academy, that I completed my high school education in 1926. There was a long family tradition at Haven—my father attended there, and so did my older sisters. It was natural for me to turn in that direction, particularly since I had no further funds to continue at Tougaloo.

While from a small boy I had been inclined toward the ministry, it was at Haven that I became completely committed to it. There were two persons who contributed considerably to my decision. One was J. Beverly F. Shaw, the president of the school, and the other was David Jordan, a teacher of history and religion.

Shaw was a very brilliant man and an inspiring speaker. He was the chapel speaker most of the time. He knew how to deal with the issues of student concern, and always left the student feeling that he or she not only could, but must, master the situations and handicaps which the black student in those days had to face. Interestingly enough, he was not overly gifted in mastering situations, but his great power of persuasion left one with the feeling that he had no other options. Dr. Shaw was not a skilled administrator. In fact, his bad management contributed to the final closing of the school in 1928.

One of the most interesting incidents that stands out in my mind was a student strike over what they said was poor food. I worked in the kitchen and got an abundance of it, but others called for a greater quantity, quality, and variety. A petition was presented to the president one day. The next morning the students assembled for breakfast, then marched out of the dining room while one of the girls played a march. No classes were attended during the day, and that night a group of the leaders went over and surrounded the president's home, making their demands from outside. The president, unfortunately, called the police (who were more than willing to come). They rounded up the students, and ordered them off the campus. This action caused problems for him that he never overcame. He later sent for the students whom he had suspended, under the condition that they would sign an apology. Some returned, but others did not.

His method of handling the aftermath was equally awkward. The vast majority of the students were poor. Although tuition, room, and board were only fourteen dollars a month, most students could not pay it without some aid; they did little jobs on the campus. Two of my sisters and I were there. I had a job which covered my expenses, except five dollars per month from my father. Each of my sisters had some work-aid on campus.

The next year, the president raised the fee to eighteen dollars and took away the jobs from all the students. That fall, only about one-third of all the students returned. The rest went to other schools. At that time, my father was serving a church at Enterprise, Mississippi. (We moved every two years. The family was large and the congregations were usually willing to share us after that time.) I came down to Meridian on the day school opened, to try to find a job in the city. I returned home that evening and reported to the family the tragic plight in which I found the school. As sad as it was, my younger sister, Juanita, and I introduced a little levity into it. She helped me to sum up the situation in the following lines (the title taken from an old song).

"I Ain't Looking for Much Crowd"

I was out to Haven the other day,
The note was sounding loud;

The echo seemed to whisper and say
I ain't looking for much crowd.

As I approached the college grounds
And the buildings I beheld;
I was startled when I looked and found
That only few did dwell.

The teachers all were present there
With their many gifts endowed;
But with melancholy looks declared,
I ain't looking for much crowd.

They flocked in droves in years gone by,
With hearts uplifted and proud;
But now they say that board's too high,
I ain't looking for much crowd.

David Jordan was a graduate of Garrett Biblical Institute, and held an M.A. from Northwestern University—rather unusual for those days. His wife held the M.A. degree in English from Iowa State University, and was the English teacher at Haven. David was a native of Mississippi, a graduate of Haven, and a protege of Dr. Shaw. Both David and his wife were excellent teachers, and had a keen interest in student life. It was under his direction that I became president of the school YMCA, and it was in the work of the Y that I gained many rich experiences, which further clarified in my mind my call to the professional ministry.

While Dr. Shaw and Mr. Jordan were both most helpful to me, it was not long before they were in conflict with each other. After Jordan was there a year and a half, Shaw dismissed him in the middle of the year. His wife, however, completed the year, and at the end of that time the Jordans moved on, leaving many friends behind. While these two men were distinctly different, and neither was flawless, they made a marvelous impact upon my life. They never reached the goals they espoused for students, but each in his own way widened the horizons of many of us. It was the inspiration I gained from these two persons which led me to begin to understand what it means to "love the Lord thy God with all thy *mind.*"

I must go back to the fall of 1925, on the day I returned to Meridian in search of a job. I met Samuel Johnson, who already had a job in the city, and knew a woman who lived one block from where he worked, who was looking for a boy to work for her. He took me out to her home. Mrs. Fritz gave me the job. She managed a rooming house where several teachers and other professional people lived. My job was primarily to make the fires in the heaters and fireplaces in the mornings, and bring in the fuel each evening for the next morning. For this service she paid me with meals and three dollars a week. The cook and her children lived in the little house in the backyard, so there was no place for me to sleep. The woman Sam worked for had a room over her garage for which she charged each of us fifty cents each week. It was completely empty and there were no toilet facilities. You can imagine how we handled it. We bought cots, and a little coal stove, and occasionally we *bought* some coal. The roof leaked, and at times we found ice on the floor in the morning. But we survived it for six months, and he and I are yet alive.

The distance from where we lived and worked to Haven was three miles. There were times when we walked to and from school twice a day—in the morning for school, return for work in the afternoon; then back to Haven for some affair in the evening and return for the night. This was twelve miles a day. The walk became a little strenuous after I became president of the senior class, as well as president of the YMCA. Evening meetings also became more frequent. We bought used bicycles. My bike did not have any brakes on it, so it was rather hazardous riding through the heavy traffic, especially in those early days when I was just learning to ride a bicycle. It was providential that I never had an accident.

There were times when Sam and I made the long trip to the campus for a meeting of the Y when we were the only two present, but we never got discouraged. David Jordan helped us to keep up the spirit.

One of the most humbling experiences I have ever had was at Haven. Even in those days, it was difficult to win a popularity contest if one lived off the campus and worked, and was professionally interested in religion. Someone sent Dr. Shaw a check to be given to "the most promising student attending Haven." At one of the chapel services he had the students nominate and elect the recipient. About ten persons were nominated. When the student body, by an overwhelming majority, selected me, I was almost moved to tears. In difficult moments since those days when one might have been inclined to give up, I have always kept the vision of the cloud of witnesses who believed in me, whose trust I dare not violate.

The work at Mrs. Fritz's continued. She was a woman of considerable kindness, although she was a child of the culture of the Old South. She encouraged me in my educational pursuits, and helped me in various ways from time to time, which did not always endear me to the other servants around the house.

Her young son, Tommy, was having difficulty with his second-year Latin. One day he and a friend of his were trying to translate a passage in Caesar while I was in the room attending to the fire. They thought they would have a little fun by asking me to read it. It happened that languages were always easy for me to grasp, and I had a special interest in Caesar's Gallic wars. I was a year ahead of Tommy, and had already covered that work. When they saw the ease with which I could read it, Tommy ran and got his mother. Mrs. Fritz asked me to be Tommy's tutor; in exchange for this favor she lightened my work load. How could Tommy ever let his comrades know that a black boy was his tutor? I knew his dilemma and struggle, and tried to help him overcome it. I think he resented it somewhat, but with my help, he at least passed the course.

Those were days in which the best white people believed that the blacks—all blacks—were inherently inferior to whites, especially in matters of intellect. Mrs. Fritz had to represent the Old South at its best to have acknowledged, under any circumstances and at whatever peril, that any black boy could teach her son. I am confident that she would have done much more for me had she not been restrained by southern mores and the fear of reprisals.

IV

College

The time for graduation from Haven came and the next move was a most important one in my mind. There was no money for college, yet I felt I had to go. Dr. Dempster D. Martin, a professor of Gammon Theological Seminary, Atlanta, came to Haven recruiting students for the seminary. He told us of a plan that Clark College and Gammon Theological Seminary had worked out, in which a student could take courses at both schools simultaneously, and do the combined seven years work in six, with a college major in Christian Education. The only expenses at Gammon were room and board. Tuition was free. Gammon students could take Clark courses on a reciprocal basis. Since they were on adjoining campuses, it made a very convenient arrangement.

I arrived at Gammon the fall of 1926, after having promised President George H. Trevor that I would bring or secure one hundred dollars during the year. When I arrived I had only seventeen dollars. He refused to talk to me at first, but I tried to convince him that more money might be forthcoming during the year. He took very little comfort in my argument, but I sensed in what he did not say, that I could probably stay. He had promised me some work, but not enough to pay the whole amount.

The students who worked in the dining room, waiting tables and washing dishes, received their room and board, but these jobs traditionally went to advanced students. I was only a beginner, and only recently a high school graduate. I had hardly reached my room when the dining room steward knocked on my door, and asked if I wanted to wait tables until the older students arrived. He made it clear that the job was temporary. I knew that I had to keep it in order to stay in school, so I approached it with that determination. The steward soon observed my knowledge of the work and the manner in which I went about it. I overheard the cook say to the steward, "You ought to try to keep that fellow." I acted as though I did not hear him, but I increased my efforts to satisfy them with my work. The president never sent for me, so I stayed the whole semester. At the beginning of the second semester, I was made head waiter, a job I held for the remainder of the school term and the entire next year.

The following year, I was placed in complete charge of the dining room. From my entrance until graduation, I worked there and covered my expenses. It is easy to feel that hard work kept me there, but as I look back over it, I am convinced that God had a hand in it. I was only a part-time student, filling a job which had always been given to full-time students, or to men who had already completed their college work.

I found the courses of study intriguing, and also the idea that I could eliminate one year. This would be slightly easier than trying to finance my education through a seven-year period. The maximum student work load was eighteen hours in each institution. Persons combining the work were supposed to take no more than a total of eighteen hours from both institutions. But while this was the plan, the registration was not carefully monitored, and one could register for the maximum in each institution. Because the students were left somewhat on their own, I found myself carrying the maximum hours in each school. It was not long before other students began trying the same thing. After a year, some of them began to fail miserably, and the practice was checked. While I was no longer allowed to carry the double load, I had already done two years in one. I was not denied the credit for the courses I had taken, and I reduced the six years to five.

It happened that I completed all my work in the Gammon Theological Seminary curriculum one year before my college work had been finished. There was a tiny church in Worcester, Massachusetts, which had been traditionally supplied by black students attending the School of Theology at Boston. The congregation had grown weary of that arrangement, and requested a pastor who could live among them. The faculty at Gammon was asked for a recommendation. My name was submitted to the district superintendent, since I could hold the church and complete my college work at Clark University, Worcester, Massachusetts. They would raise the salary from six hundred dollars to twelve hundred dollars and furnish a parsonage. I had accepted it, but the final arrangements were delayed and by the time the district superintendent had worked them out, I had decided to decline the offer.

As busy as the work and academic programs kept me, there was still time for romance, for it was in Atlanta that Annie Belle Thaxton and I first met in 1927. She had completed the two-year college program at Clark the year I arrived and was on her first teaching post in McDonough, now less than twenty miles from Atlanta. She came to Atlanta one weekend as a house guest of one of her friends who was a member of Providence Baptist Church. The church was just a few blocks from the Gammon campus, and I worshipped there occasionally. We met that Sunday at Providence. The name was perhaps more appropriate to describe our meeting than it was for the church. I knew from the moment I saw Belle that she was the girl for me, and now fifty years later, I am more convinced of it than ever before. We were married, July 18, 1929, two years after we first met.

There was a rule at Gammon that any student who came to the seminary single, had to get the permission of the faculty to marry while still in school. When we decided to get married, I did not request faculty permission. At the time of registration, the registrar inquired, Are you single or married?" My reply was, "I'm married, Doctor." There was no further comment, and it brought to an end any further effort to enforce on any student an age-old policy that had outlived its day. We believed that we knew what we were doing, and subsequent events proved that we were right, for we both went on to complete college and university work, finding marriage an asset rather than a liability.

The year 1929 was a memorable one for us, for it was that year that I joined the North Carolina Annual Conference as a probationary member. There were a number of students at Gammon from North Carolina who became friends of mine, and Robert N. Brooks, later Bishop Brooks, a teacher at Gammon, was a member of that conference. He was an exceedingly polished and impressive person. One day he talked to me about my future and suggested that I might enjoy being a member of the North Carolina Conference. I was highly pleased with the suggestion and followed through on it.

I finished the work at Gammon in 1930, but had another year to finish in college before the degrees, A.B. and B.D. would be conferred. This was a crucial moment. There was no longer a reason to hold the job at Gammon, and entirely new arrangements had to be made if I were to return to Clark College, Atlanta.

Dr. Willis J. King, later Bishop King, had just been elected president of Samuel Huston College—now Huston-Tillotson, Austin, Texas. Dr. King had just returned from a sabbatical which he spent at Oxford University. He had been my teacher at Gammon. He was a man dedicated to learning, and sought to encourage a love for learning among his students. I was impressed by his outlook, for he was a remarkable teacher.

Many of the public schools in West Texas for blacks left much to be desired. Samuel Huston established a one-year remedial program for students who had graduated from substandard high schools; it was called the sub-college department. Dr. King offered me a job as head of that department, in exchange for my expenses, which I gladly accepted. Things went well, and I graduated in the spring of 1931. Samuel Huston and Gammon conferred the degrees.

While Dr. King was an excellent teacher, he was not a skilled administrator. His administrative weaknesses included making decisions before he thoroughly thought them through, and his inability to stand by them.

Austin, Texas was a long way from High Point, North Carolina, where the Annual Conference of 1931 was to be held, and where I might be given an appointment. This was in the heart of the depression and the conference would not convene until November. Jobs were almost impossible to get, so we had two problems—survival for the summer and transportation to North Carolina.

There was a hot dog stand on the campus called the Dragon Inn, named for the football team. The student who ran it went into bankruptcy. One of the reasons was that he put the little box in which he kept his money under the counter— within reach of the students. The old trick was to order a hamburger, and while Jerry was preparing it, to reach under the counter and get the change to pay for it. While this was meant as just a mischievous stunt, it destroyed his business.

The college charged a rental fee of five dollars a month for the inn. Belle and I took it over a little after the second semester began. We started with practically no money. The first day we replaced the hamburger meat as we sold it. At the end of the day we had made thirty-five dollars. That was a windfall in those days. From that time on we were in business. It was the rendezvous for students and faculty.

We hired one of the bright young students, whom I was teaching, to take care of the inn in the evenings. The evenings had been some of our best hours, but business began to fall off. One problem was that he closed frequently before time; the other was that he added water to the milk, and kept for himself the returns on the extra pints and quarts thus available. He also bought his own supplies and sold them instead of selling ours. We discovered all this before he had time to do much harm.

We were doing so well that the president suggested that we move into a larger space and take care of the food for the summer school, since the dining room would not be open and food would not be available elsewhere. We were thrilled over the prospects and bought silver and dishes to accommodate the people. The business was most profitable for the first few days, but suddenly it declined. We could not imagine what was happening. We soon discovered that the president's daughters had established a food stand just in front of the door of the building where the classes were held. Customers had to come across the campus to get to us. The president admitted that it was wrong, but that family pressure had goaded him into it. I do not think he ever felt right about it.

Belle and I felt that we shouldn't be in competition with the president's family, so we closed the inn. After telling the president exactly what I thought of his action, we left without further ado.

V

My First Appointment

En route to North Carolina, we spent one month with my family in Montrose, Mississippi, and one month with Belle's family in McDonough, Georgia.

When we reached Atlanta, it was almost a "thumb-a-ride" to High Point where the conference was held. Appointment prospects were poor. There were six of us coming from Gammon for our first appointments. The depression was taking its toll everywhere, and even the best churches were only able to pay very little. Some medical doctors had to take much of their fees in produce, and teachers were paid in scrip (money in which use was limited to food and other urgent commodities). While I was admitted into full membership and ordained an elder, there was no assurance that I would get an appointment wherein Belle and I would have a reasonable chance to survive. While every preacher was entitled to an appointment, there was nothing in the rules that said what kind of an appointment it would be. There was no such thing as minimum salary; except in another sense, that all salaries were minimum.

It was Sunday morning, just before the appointments were read, that the district superintendent came and told me that I would be appointed to Kernersville. I was greatly pleased, for it was situated in the general vicinity of Greensboro, High Point, and Winston-Salem. The conference journal listed the annual salary as seven hundred dollars, and there was no parsonage.

We can never forget this first little church. Kernersville was scarcely more than a village. Seven miles out in the country was New Bethel, a part of the Kernersville charge where the pastor went twice a month in the afternoon for service. As I look back now, I know how kind the congregations were to us. We were young and inexperienced. The charge had been accustomed to older preachers who lived in their own homes and came for worship services on Sunday, to conduct funerals, and other special occasions. They rented a house for us (considered nice for those days), and furnished it by collecting different items from members of the congregation, which had been stored for one reason or another. When they got it all together we were adequately provided for. The only flaw in the arrangement was that each time a member who provided furnishing became disenchanted, she came and collected the items which belonged to her. Fortunately there were always others who would replace them.

There were a number of snares in that first official board meeting, but there were enough good people to help keep the organization on a steady course. I can never forget the name of Isabella Bost, the widow of a minister who lived in Kernersville. She was one of the most remarkable persons I have ever known. She was at that first meeting, and in a quiet and unobtrusive way, helped to guide it to the right conclusions. There were others who also wanted it to succeed.

Kernersville had many young people who helped to give vitality to the church. A number of them graduated from colleges and universities and presently are holding prominent positions in North Carolina and other places.

Our daughter was born in Kernersville, and we named her after the woman we revered so much, Isabella. In fact, we named her for three members—Isabella, Vera, and Marilla, all of whom we remember with deep affection.

I had plenty of help in those days. One of the old pastors returned frequently, visited members, advised them on procedures, and made himself available for funerals and weddings. While the congregation was very supportive of me, these functions were all conducted by former pastors. Of course, it was a learning experience for me, for in all my ministry I have never gone back to a church I served to take charge of a funeral nor to give a commencement address at a school. I learned that when the bishop appointed me *to* a church, he also appointed me *from* a church that I was to leave alone. Some preachers never learn that lesson.

Our first year at Kernersville came to a close, and the district superintendent, Robert W. Winchester, a wise and venerable man and lifetime friend, was convinced that, as much as we liked Kernersville, it was wrong to keep us at a charge where it was such a struggle to make ends meet. While the salary was set at $700, we had actually received for the year $324. The people were kind, however, and shared with us their food and firewood. We went through the year, uncomplaining about finances or voicing other deprivations we endured.

The first car I owned was purchased there. It was a 1919 Model T Ford. The sale price was twenty-five dollars. I did not have the five-dollar down payment, so one of the church members who worked at the garage paid it for me. My obligation was to pay the other twenty dollars, at the rate of five dollars a month. I know now what a sacrifice it was for that member to have paid the first five dollars.

I had the suspicion that part of the decision of my district superintendent was based on his feeling that my idealism and exacting administration would be a bit strenuous, in the long run, on a charge that had been free to drift in all sorts of directions, due to absentee administrations. For example, I refused to recommend the renewal of the licenses of the two local preachers, because they had been ineffective. They had just been allowed to drift along through the years, and the annual renewal of their licenses was automatic.

The Kernersville Church owned a cemetery which the trustees placed in the hands of a committee to sell plots. In practice, the committee was not accountable to anyone, and had not made a report on the finances in years. When I called for a report, they fumbled, so I unilaterally dissolved the committee, and ordered the trustees to assume direct responsibility for the cemetery and make an annual report to the Fourth Quarterly Conference (now known as the Charge Conference). This was a most sensitive matter since it involved some of the prominent families of the church.

I must say a few words about New Bethel Church. It was a small rural church, and was almost inaccessible. I shall never forget straddling ruts that were five and six feet deep in our Model T Ford. I would always have Belle get out of the car and walk up the hill so that at least one of us would have a survivor's chance. The margin for error was small, and the slightest misjudgment in driving could have been disastrous. We soon learned how to survive, and to take it in stride.

Some experiences at New Bethel were unforgettable. I remember that first Sunday afternoon. We arrived at the church around 2:30 for the 3:00 p.m. service, but it was not until 3:30 that the first family came. They drove their mule, hitched to a wagon. That was the general mode of transportation in that little community, especially for those who lived too far to walk. It was 4:00 p.m. before enough people had arrived for me to attempt to open the service. I had been taught at the theological seminary never to begin a worship service late—a principle I have always sought to hold onto religiously—but New Bethel had to be an exception this first Sunday. There were no hymnals, nor musical instruments, and I could not lead a hymn, although I knew many of them by memory. In those days, many people did, for hymn books were not available in numerous small rural churches. I tried to think of the most familiar hymn I knew with the hope that someone in the congregation would lead it. I recall that this was a cold November Sunday, and we were all gathered around a little potbellied stove as the worship service began. With great trepidation, I said, "Let us begin the service by singing hymn number 291, 'O For a Thousand Tongues to Sing.' Will one of you lead it?"

They wouldn't buy that one. They wanted to hear their new preacher sing. They claimed to have colds and couldn't lead it. Although I had never done it before, I pitched it myself. By the time I got as far along as "O for a Thou——," an old brother took it away from me, and the service continued.

Another New Bethel experience I recall is a baptism service. All the candidates for baptism wanted to be immersed, so I acceded to their desires. The water available was a large spring of cold, flowing water. The idea came to me that it would be impressive to give the homily while standing in the middle of the pool prior to the ceremony. The service went well, but the aftermath was horrible. I could hardly talk when it was over; I had contracted one of the most severe colds of my lifetime. This was my last participation in a baptism by immersion.

The church in Kernersville had a choir. Some of these members had very good voices, but they did not take well to pastoral suggestions concerning the music they sang or the people who sang in it. There was a young woman who had one of the best voices in the town whom they would not include because she did not live on the right side of the tracks. I intervened, and the choir struck. (There were strikes long before there were labor unions.) The strike went on for two Sundays. No one said anything, but no one went into the choir stand. I acted as if they were there and just went on with the service. I led a hymn one day, and a young woman in the congregation giggled. I turned around and said, "Martha, will you lead this hymn?"

She said, "I can't."

I said, "Well, don't laugh at me," and kept on singing.

During the two-week choir strike, an embarrassing incident occurred in the community in which some of the members were involved. The next Sunday, everybody was back in the choir. They apologized and promised never to strike again. It later became a joke.

VI

Life in Greensboro

We reluctantly went from Kernersville to the northwest Greensboro charge. Though it was small, we felt that the promises were great. There were three churches and a much larger membership.

The little parsonage and one of the churches were located just a few yards outside the Greensboro city limits, which was three miles from the center of the city. My predecessor lived in his own home in town, and the little parsonage, built out of used lumber, had never been occupied. Air conditioning was neither vogueish nor necessary. The place was well ventilated. Air entered from all directions. Belle and I shut out most of the air by papering the house with large white second sheets that were given to us from the printing press, and by putting linoleum rugs on the floors. They could be bought for one dollar down and another dollar a week until paid for. Fortunately we managed to make our regular payments. The charge bought us used furniture, and Belle, Isabella, and I were off to a happy start.

The congregations were loyal and soon made adjustments to their young ministerial family. The people were poor, but they shared with the church what they had with complete abandon. The chances for a better livelihood had greatly improved with the new parish, although the actual cash salary was hardly more than double. The people were highly evangelical in their preference, but accepted their young

42

pastor of a more subdued nature with warmth and sometimes enthusiasm. We served there for three years.

The charge included three churches—Mt. Carmel, Warren Street, and Mt. Tabor. Mt. Carmel was the church where the parsonage was located and was about an eighth of a mile from the bus line to the central section of the city. The location was convenient, and bus fare was only five cents, but the depression was at its depth, so Belle and I took turns walking to and from the city, and rode the bus only when absolutely necessary. We chose to have our mail come to a box at the post office instead of having it delivered RFD. This meant a daily trip to the post office, which was sixty cents a week—a coveted sum then. Walking was a lot of fun in those days. I sold the old Ford we had in Kernersville, and it was more than a year before we could afford to buy another one. This was years before jogging became popular. Our exercise was functional.

The next car we bought was a Model T Ford Sedan. We paid ten dollars for it with the license tag on it. At that time the tag alone would have cost twelve dollars and fifty cents. One day we started to drive it to McDonough, Georgia, Belle's hometown, about four hundred miles away. The generator which furnished the energy for the lights went bad enroute, so we stopped at a garage in Spartanburg, South Carolina to have it repaired. The man sold me a used one, which ceased to operate after a few miles. When we examined it, we discovered that in spite of the fact that he had brought another one out of the garage, he reinstalled our old generator and charged us for another one. Since the car would run without the generator we just kept going. Belle's mother was seriously ill, and it was urgent that we arrive as soon as possible. As we look back, we marvel that we made the trip at all, much less between sunrise and sunset. We didn't know any better than to try, and the Lord sustained us.

Greensboro holds for us fond memories and interesting experiences. I remember my first arrival at Warren Street Church. It was a Sunday morning, just in time for the 11:00

a.m. service. I had carefully prepared my sermon to deliver at that occasion; but this was not to be. A member of the congregation had died, and the family had the funeral planned for that hour. Another minister was there to give the eulogy. I was asked to preside. This was a bit disconcerting, but I never indicated it. I did make sure, however, that I was brought in on the planning of all funerals from that time on.

One member of the congregation resented having the funeral at the regular worship hour, and publicly said so. It created a real controversy that Sunday morning, and there were scars in relationships between that member and the bereaved family that never healed. I managed to stay out of the fight, but the occasion gave me an opportunity to set up a system in which matters like this would always be cleared with the pastor so there would not be a recurrence of incidents like this one.

This family became some of our warmest friends and we still remember them with deep affection.

I recall an incident that occurred at Mt. Carmel, the church where the parsonage was located. A barefoot prophet and his barefoot wife had informed a member of the congregation that God had revealed to him a message of evils which would befall the church, and had commissioned him and his wife to proclaim the message that evening at exactly 8:00 p.m. He had to deliver it exactly at that moment, he said, or God would withdraw the message. I was greatly surprised to hear the announcement. My only response was that God had given me a message to deliver to the congregation exactly at the same time, and as pastor, I was under obligation to do it.

The prophet and his wife made their appearance. They were seated in the front pew. The church was crowded—one of the largest congregations I ever had. I began my sermon at 7:45, in order to be ahead of the prophet, and when 8:00 p.m. came I was still preaching—the sermon went thirty minutes longer than usual. The audience was the coldest I have ever addressed, but I saw no option but to keep on going until the prophet's moment of inspiration had passed. Following the sermon, I proceeded with the service, and the prophet did not make any attempt to speak. Those wonderful people did not hold it against me for long.

Early in my ministry, there was a young man in my church about my age, who appeared profoundly religious—an officer in the church. He sat in what was commonly known as the Amen Corner, where the brothers and sisters gave vocal sanction to the preacher when he said something in his sermon that they felt moved to support.

One Sunday morning, just before I extended the invitation to Holy Communion, he indicated he had something he would like to say to the congregation. I was sure that it was a word of endorsement. How often a young pastor feels that need! But I was shocked when he took a different course: "I have been greatly moved by the sermons our pastor has been preaching," he began. "Each one seemed to have struck me directly. They have made me feel unworthy. I do not feel that I am worthy of being a steward in this church any longer, so I am resigning this morning." It seemed appropriate to me to merely extend the invitation to Holy Communion, which read in part: "Ye that do truly and earnestly repent of your sins . . . and intend to lead a new life . . . draw near with faith and take this holy Sacrament to your comfort . . ." He was one of the first to receive the Communion.

He continued to serve his church and never mentioned the matter again. There must have been something that he misunderstood, and I was too inexperienced to have pursued the matter privately with him. It may have been that my sermons did not carry with them enough of the element of hope and of God's reconciling and forgiving love. Or, this may have been his way of reaching out for help. In my more mature years, I have often wished that I had sought a chance to hear him out, and had been more of a shepherd to a man who was seeking to find his way.

Mt. Carmel had some of the most dedicated people in official positions I have ever known. A number of them, however, were very literal in their interpretation of the

Scriptures and what they felt the Scriptures imply. The program of the church was completely adult centered, with nothing directed toward the interests of youth and children except within an adult framework. Belle and I sought to organize some recreational activities. Among them was a baseball team. Some of the elders thought it was a sin to play baseball, and challenged me in an official board meeting. In the midst of the discussion, a very devout man who had driven a V8 Ford to church that evening, said, "Jesus never played baseball." I said, "That's probably true, but he never drove a V8 either." After hearty laughter the matter dropped and was never brought up again.

I learned early that a sense of humor can be a reconciling force when it is used lovingly and appropriately. Some people have that gift and grace and others do not. If humor does not come naturally, one should not try to use it. Attempts at it that do not go across can be embarrassing and may even backfire.

Greensboro was somewhat of an educational center. Women's College, of the University of North Carolina, and Greensboro College for Women of the (then) Methodist Episcopal Church, South, were there, but neither was open to blacks. In fact, no white college or university in the South was open to people of color. But there was also Agricultural and Technical College—a state institution—and Bennett College. Bennett College, founded in 1873 by the Freedmen's Society, operated as a coeducational institution until 1926. The school was not doing well, and the Woman's Home Missionary Society saw an opportunity to develop a college with standards of excellence for the education of black women in the South. It was done in cooperation with the Board of Education of the Methodist Episcopal Church.

The primary success of this newly founded institution was due to two factors: The ardent support of the Woman's Home Missionary Society, later the Woman's Division of Christian Service, and the election of David Dallas Jones as its first president. It was under his administration that this school, with unpromising and difficult beginnings, became one of the best colleges in the country.

We came to Greensboro when Bennett was six years old. It was struggling for survival. A fund raising campaign had been conducted in the city and pledges were made by individuals and businesses before the crash of 1929. Most of them were yet unpaid. President Jones asked me if I would be willing to try to collect some of them during my spare time. I consented. He invited me to his office, gave me a pep talk, and handed me a list of the pledges. I left with considerable enthusiasm, but by the time I reached the office of the first prospect, I had begun to ponder the realities of my almost impossible task. After passing the office door several times, I had built up enough nerve to go in. To my surprise, I met a very gracious and understanding man who, while he did not give me a check, gave me a promise. The ice was broken, and I found the job fascinating, not begging, but urging persons to make investments in a worthy institution. Later I discovered that President Jones had not believed the pledges could be collected; but in time, most of the people honored them. This was the beginning, not only of a lasting friendship, but also of later decisions I was called on to make concerning the future of my ministry.

One had to be ingenious during those depression days, as a means of survival. Belle had taken a course from the American School of Home Economics in making Fanny Farmer candies. (I can still taste the penuche, so smooth there was no feeling of graininess on the tongue.) We started producing them on a small scale, but they sold so fast that we employed agents on a commission basis. The business went well; we were patronized by many people across the town. Some wanted to make investments in it, but we decided to keep it private.

VII

On to Thomasville

In 1934 I was appointed to a church in Thomasville, North Carolina, about twenty-five miles from Greensboro. We were not happy to leave Greensboro, but the cabinet insisted that they had an awkward situation in Thomasville, which only a man of my leadership ability could handle. I later found that they were really trying to open up a place in Greensboro for an elderly man who wanted to be near home.

Thomasville was not without its problems. The church had built a beautiful eight-room parsonage on a lot which a society had given it forty years earlier, when it had discontinued its existence. The building of the parsonage had been financed by the company that constructed it, and when payments continued to lag, the company threatened to foreclose and sue the trustees. The church appealed to the bank for a loan, but in investigating the deeds, the bank discovered they were not signed by all of the previous trustees of the society, and were therefore not valid. The task before us was to validate the deeds and secure the loan. There is a long story behind it, but in time it was done and the loan was secured.

The challenge in Thomasville was the number of young people who needed some opportunities for creativity and self-expression. The churches and the school building were all that were available for any of them, whatever their color.

St. John's Church had the advantage of having the use of the old church building which was just behind the new church, and had been used by the city for additional classrooms for the public school. The city was just completing the building of a new school with adequate space for its program and no longer needed our building. With the help of the Women's Society of the white Methodist Church in Thomasville and the merchants and businessmen of the city, we were able to open up at the old church building, the first cultural and recreational building in town.

Thomasville was a furniture center and most of the men who had jobs worked in this industry. Volunteers from among them helped to build the equipment we needed. There were sewing rooms where the girls could be taught, and because the merchants had made the materials available, the girls not only learned to make clothing, but were able to keep for themselves the garments they had made. A reading room was provided, and books and publications were collected from the community by the women.

The outdoor program provided for a variety of recreation. Five and six hundred young people gathered at the center evenings from five to nine. Each Sunday afternoon, large crowds met at the church for a religious program. It was as a result of this movement that the city organized its first recreational center.

St. John's Church, Thomasville, was the seat of the 1936 Annual Conference. This was quite a chore. The people were housed in homes, and the hosts entertained them as a courtesy. The conference began on a Monday and closed on Sunday. It was looked upon as an honor to entertain an annual conference, and it usually went to the churches where the older men were pastors. Nevertheless, when it was over I felt like the man who was being ridden out of town on a fence rail.

"Gentlemen," the man said, "except for the honor of it, I would just as soon not have had the ride."

Belle's feeling was different than mine. She said she enjoyed it.

Annual conferences were usually rather dull affairs, except

a few inspirational addresses and the bishop's Sunday sermon. Since the appointments could be shifted on the platform, even after the sermon, it was sometimes difficult for one to keep his mind on holy things during the delivery of the sermon.

Still there were occasional sessions where great issues were discussed. The Conference of 1936 was one of them. It was the year following the General Conference, which had voted on the merger of the Methodist Episcopal Church, the Methodist Episcopal Church, South, and the Protestant Methodist Church. The annual conferences had to ratify the action for final approval.

The problem of what would happen to the Negro Annual Conference was at stake. Prior to the merger in 1939, all the Negro annual conferences were in the Methodist Episcopal Church. The merger proposal was to have five geographical jurisdictions and a sixth jurisdiction based on race. Once the plan was designed black protest made little significant difference; but the black conferences debated the issues, nevertheless, and their delegates made their views known at the General Conference.

The conferences which later became the Central Jurisdiction were overwhelmingly opposed (16 of the 19 that existed at that time), but that made no difference whatever. Those of us who were old enough to participate in the movement at any level looked upon it as an abandonment of the blacks by the church—in which we placed our hopes.

We argued that the Central Jurisdiction would be humiliating and dehumanizing. It locked segregation in the constitution of the church, and made it hopelessly difficult to change the constitution. It robbed the blacks of a sense of dignity, and placed them on the defensive with black denominations who had refused to accept such indignities. It robbed the white church of its best opportunity to be the true church of Christ, at a time when the nation desperately needed its leadership and example.

It was such a debate that took place in the North Carolina

Conference in 1936. While this was not the beginning of segregated Negro annual conferences, it was the first time segregation had been written into the constitution of the church. It was difficult to understand how otherwise good people could have been so insensitive at this point. Bishop Wallace E. Brown, for example, who presided at the conference, almost threatened the preachers who dared to speak against the proposal. Nevertheless, some of us maintained opposition to the plan.

VIII

Back to School

During our stay in Thomasville, President Jones continued to discuss with me the possibility of joining the staff at Bennett. Belle and I prayed over the matter and felt that at the time we should stay with the church. We did come to the conclusion, however, that we would be better servants of the whole church if we had a broader educational horizon. This was in 1937. The depression had not been overcome, and we did not have the money to live in New York, to say nothing of paying fees at Union Theological Seminary and Columbia University. We decided, even so, to take an adventure in faith. There were a few vague promises, but nothing concrete. Our colleagues in the conference thought we were mentally ill. Perhaps there is a fine line between faith and illness. When one wins, we say it was faith; when one loses, we say the venture was foolish.

We arrived at the psychological moment. Dr. Frederick B. Newell, then executive secretary of the New York City Society of the New York Annual Conference (later Bishop Newell), was looking for someone to supervise a little mission house, which housed a nursery school—an effort at an organized church. The compensation was an apartment in the house. A place to live was quite important. Because women could get jobs more easily than men, Belle worked, and by careful planning we were able to meet our bills.

When the time came for registration, I had to make the decision between a narrow, specialized education, and one with a broader sphere. For help in making this decision, I owe much to Dr. David Roberts who was dean of students at Union Theological Seminary. My college major was Christian education, with thirty hours of seminary work counting toward it. The Christian education program at Union was a combined one with Columbia University, under the faculties of political science, pure science and philosophy. That meant two years of study for the M.A. degree instead of one, because my college background was lacking in such courses as economics, history, philosophy, and political science.

On the other hand, I could go directly to Teachers College, Columbia, with a major in Christian education and do the work in one year. I hesitated, for it would mean an extra year that I felt I could not afford to spend. David Roberts advised that I should, and Belle insisted that I must go to Union. I have always been grateful to them both that I did, for it gave me the background I needed for a sound education and for the doctoral program which I pursued later at New York University.

It gave me the opportunity also, to study under such persons as Henry P. Van Dusen, Reinhold Niebuhr, Frederick Grant, Robert E. Hume, and Harrison Elliot of Union; and Harry Carmen and Charles A. Beard of Columbia. These teachers and others did much to give me a new and broadened perspective. To have a great teacher is one of the greatest treasures one can be given. While they were all highly gifted, they varied widely in the way they made their contributions. Niebuhr, for example, was a most impressive teacher and one could hardly wait to get to his lectures. The students used to say, "Thou shall love the Lord thy God, and thy Niebuhr as thyself."

Grant was a great New Testament scholar, a prolific writer, and was good in a question-and-answer setting; but rather dull in a classroom lecture. Some of the students facetiously referred to his courses as Grant's Tomb, but the student who took him seriously could find his courses highly rewarding. He wrote with great skill and erudition.

It was scholars like these who taught me how to be brave enough to place all issues under the searchlight of truth and follow where the evidence seems to lead. I had considerable trouble in the early stages, in questioning every issue, and at the same time holding onto my faith—a faith that had accepted easy and uncritical answers as absolutes. The courses and teachers at Union were disturbing at times, because some of them raised issues that I had never faced before, although the professors were generally reassuring.

I remember a course in philosophy at Columbia under a professor who was a naturalist. Almost everything he taught was contrary to that which I held sacred. He sensed it by the questions I raised and the responses I made. One day he invited me to his home and we talked for more than an hour. He assured me that he was not trying to rob me of my beliefs, but they were just not his beliefs. While there was seldom a time when we were in agreement on any point of view, there was always a meeting of spirits after that conversation in his home. He was always interested in hearing my positions, and frequently referred to me in class.

I began to learn that the community of understanding is on the level of the spirit. I had been facing the question, How does one deal with a mix that will not mix? It can be a most frustrating experience. There is always the temptation to shut one's mind, close out opposing views, abandon one's view for the opposing one, or take what is commonly called the eclectic approach—that is, select what seems best from each system. In that there is always the danger, however, of selecting views that end in a hodgepodge of contradictions. One college student I knew solved her dilemma by giving up all her beliefs.

Those days at Union and Columbia were of great value to me because they forced me to critically examine my own faith, and to reconstruct it on what has been a solid foundation for many years. I am firmly convinced that when one's faith has to be sheltered from any ideologies in order to remain firm, it needs reexamining and reconstructing. The experience helped me further to understand people who have faced and are facing the struggle to get their bearings, and frequently to assist them in doing it.

The first semester of 1940, I matriculated in the school of education, New York University, as a Doctor of Education candidate. This work was interrupted at the end of the semester, however, which will be discussed later. I completed the remainder of the residence requirements during summers and was awarded the degree in 1948.

My experiences at NYU were vastly different from those at Union and Columbia. Those were the years when I was entering into a new world and required a reorientation toward life, as well as building a solid academic foundation for scholarly pursuits. This had been done by the time I reached NYU. I met there also some professors of spirits kindred with my own. I shall mention only two of them. The man who was my advisor was Samuel Hamilton. He was a Methodist preacher, highly respected in the field of Christian education, and guided a number of students through doctoral programs. Several of these students later distinguished themselves as scholars and church leaders. While he was a good teacher, his most outstanding quality was his ability to inspire students to be both competent and committed. They regarded him as a professor who was a friend in the most genuine sense.

I can never forget two conferences I had with Professor Hamilton. The first one was when I went down to the school to matriculate. After having talked with me at length, he turned to me with a smile and said: "We are glad to have you come to NYU." And then he said: "I think I should say to you that some universities make it easier for Negroes to get doctorates than for whites, and some make it more difficult. Here we do neither. We have one standard for all."

The other conversation took place in his office the evening before my final oral examination. He seemed a bit ill at ease. I wondered what was wrong. I do not know if he was remembering what he said when I registered in 1940 or felt the situation had changed. He strolled across the floor with a pensive look on his face. He finally asked, "Prince Albert, can I say something to you?" I replied, "Surely, anything you wish to say."

He said, "You know, this ought not to be true, but it is. A Negro has to know twice as much as a white man to be considered equal to him. Don't forget that tomorrow morning when you come in here for your oral."

When the committee highly commended me on my performance, he was one of the happiest and most relieved persons in the world. His face literally shone. He was proud that the committee had dealt with me without prejudice, and that I had not let him down. He had gone out on the limb with this black man (me), and at the psychological moment he was not sure that, against his greatest hopes, being black, even at NYU, would not make a difference.

Dr. Herman Harrell Horne was the other professor who still stands out in my memory. He was one of the best teachers I have ever known. While the course I took with him was the philosophy of education, he had the reputation of making any course he taught interesting. He had a way of taking difficult concepts and discussing them in such simple and intriguing ways. He knew how to make the most timid student become a participator, and at the same time keep the most aggressive student in balance. He insisted on each student becoming an independent thinker.

His reputation with students on oral doctoral exams was outstanding. He was said to have been able to give the weak candidate just enough assurance to help him through, and give the cocky student enough difficulty to help him or her realize there were many things yet to be learned. I am among the many students who remember him with deep gratitude and affection.

IX

My Ministry as Teacher

After spending one semester at NYU, 1940, President Jones of Bennett College offered me the position of assistant to the president. I wasn't quite sure what that meant, but the title was intriguing, and it was time for us to have some relief from the struggle and financial strain of living in New York, so I gladly accepted it.

My original job was to help the president in fund raising—somewhat like a vice president in charge of development today. But as needs arose I took on additional responsibility. For example, I taught a course in religion three hours a week, acted as chaplain of the college, recruited students, and conducted a thirty-minute radio program, five days a week, and enjoyed it all.

My three years at Bennett, working with David Jones, were a continuing education. He was a most remarkable man. Although a number of teachers had difficulty adjusting to his rather exacting administration, I seemed to thrive on it. He insisted on high standards of performance for teachers and students alike. He was an exceptionally hard worker and had a low level of tolerance for those who were not.

David Jones enjoyed telling the story of a man who worked with him in the early years of the college, who felt he was working too hard and not getting the proper recognition.

"Mr. President," he said, "can't you give me a job with a little more status and a little less work?"

With the president there was no job at Bennett, from the

laundry to the office of the president, which did not have status, and there was none that did not require hard work.

As demanding as he could be at times, he had great compassion and concern for the welfare of every student. He knew each of the five hundred girls by name, and generally knew something concerning their families. He knew where every graduate was working and what each was doing. He was a stickler for time and for details. He knew how to plan and execute those plans. He was marvelous in public relations. To work closely with a man like this was a coveted privilege.

This was the heyday of Christian education, and theological seminaries were beginning to place considerable emphasis on it. The schools that had departments were trying to strengthen them, and those that did not were in the business of organizing them. Gammon Theological Seminary was just emerging from the depression. It offered courses in Christian education, but did not have such a department; it was not financially able to do so. Dr. John Q. Schisler, then the executive secretary of the Division of the Local Church of the Board of Education of the Methodist Church, made funds available through his division for a professorship in this field at Gammon.

Dr. Willis J. King, with whom I had worked at Samuel Huston College, was now president of Gammon. Although we separated at Samuel Huston College under conditions that were not the most congenial, he did offer me the job.

The seminary provided homes for all of its professors, but since this was a new department there was no home, owned by Gammon, available for the person who was to fill this post. Dr. King, in his letter, apprised me of this, but said that the home of the former president of Clark College was available, since the college had moved to the other side of town. He said the house was large, but comfortable. I accepted the offer, July 1, 1943, and moved to Atlanta, September first.

In return for the house, I would teach two courses at Clark

College, in addition to my work at Gammon. Those were the days in which teachers carried heavy loads, so I accepted it. When I arrived on campus with my personal effects, Dr. King escorted me to the house. While the van was being unloaded, he informed me that I would not occupy all the house; certain rooms in it would be reserved for guests who visited the campus. Fortunately it did not take long for me to change his mind.

While Dr. King had his personality quirks, it is only fair to say that he understood theological education, and contributed much to the progress of the school.

I had come to feel that while Christian education was one of the most demanding needs of the church, much of it was done on a surface and superficial level. As I saw it, there were two problems: one was that whereas Christian education had profited by many modern psychological insights, some of what was passing for Christian education was void of theological depth. The other problem was that many workers in the field saw Christian education as mere activity—meeting together, having recreation, and fellowship. It was the idea that keeping young people engaged in wholesome activity would in itself develop good habits and Christian living. Then too, in the teaching program, more emphasis was frequently placed on methodology than content. There is no doubt that wholesome recreation and fellowship have a tremendous amount to contribute to the Christian way of life, and better methods of communicating the gospel through the educational process are desperately needed. But recreation, however helpful, and methods, however good, can never be substitutes for substance; style cannot take the place of content, and content must always be put in the context of the Christian faith. It is content that leads to Christian experience and a Christian way of life.

Harrison Elliott, in his book, *Can Religious Education be Christian?* sought to come to grips with this problem by using the theological approach to Christian education. While questions may be raised concerning Dr. Elliott's conclusions, he examined Christian education in the light of theological presuppositions.

My lifetime convictions are that the educational work of the church is one of the chief commitments of the pastor and lay worker. So I accepted the primary task of the Department of Christian Education at Gammon—that of enabling the students to become Christian educators, primarily in the local church.

It was most encouraging to me that the Gammon students sensed early the need for a wider knowledge in this field, and while only six hours of Christian education were required for the B.D. degree, most of the students took as many of the courses as they could schedule. The degree of master of religious education (M.R.E.), a two-year course, was open only to women. Full clergy rights for women had not been granted by the church (those came in 1956), so it was assumed that women would not want to pursue a course which prepared them primarily for work that was not open to them.

Gammon had a long and distinguished history, and was singular in the education of black clergy and lay workers. The school was organized in 1883 as the Gammon School of Theology of Clark University. It became an independent theological seminary in 1888, and was named for its chief benefactor, Elijah Gammon. The significance of Gammon has to be assessed with some reflection of the responsibility which was placed upon it.

The leadership of the black preacher was conceived to be important in the solution of the problems of the newly emancipated Negro following the Civil War, and his training was indispensable. Typical of this conception was that expressed in the tenth annual report of the Freedmen's Aid Society of the (then) Methodist Episcopal Church (p. 6). "As a pure and intelligent ministry is the most essential instrumentality in the elevation of this race, to its attainment, our society has devoted especial attention." This idea was further stressed by the Reverend C. H. Payne, in an address at the dedication of the new library in 1889. "Certain it is that the ministry of the Negro race is an exceptionally potent factor in solving the destiny of that race . . ." (p. 1, History of Gammon Theological Seminary, unpublished thesis, Prince A. Taylor, Jr.). Under the impetus of this movement, classes and separate departments of theology were organized in the colleges that already existed. It was soon discovered that the arrangement was inadequate to meet the need for ministerial education, which led to the establishment of Gammon Theological Seminary.

In 1886 Gammon was a project of the Methodist Episcopal Church. Reverend Atticus G. Haygood, later Bishop Haygood, of the Methodist Episcopal Church, South, delivered the annual address for the seminary. He declared the place of Gammon to be so significant that, "It may be questioned whether any single institution, under the care of the Methodist Episcopal Church, holds a place of importance and responsibility equal to that which is possible to the Gammon School of Theology. To state the thought otherwise, the Methodist Episcopal Church could better afford to lose Drew than Gammon. Looking at the matter in another light, it may well be questioned whether any single institution in the Southern states could not be better spared . . ." Present on the platform at the following commencement exercises were, Governor H. B. McDaniel, of the state of Georgia; Dr. G. I. Orr, state school commissioner; and Judge M. W. Reese of the state supreme court (Southwestern Christian Advocate, April 15, 1886).

In 1889, the eminent poet John Greenleaf Whittier, thought so much of the aims and purpose of Gammon, and the significance of the seminary's work, that he gave the school its original motto:

> Light, Freedom, Truth, be ever
>   these thine own
> Light to see Truth, Freedom to
>   make it known:

> One Work, God's Work, our Wills
> His Will alone.

Until relatively recent years the vast majority of the black pastors and many leaders in education, as well as general officers of the church, received their basic theological education at Gammon. Gammon had a special and most difficult mission when one considers the educational distance the black clergy had to travel in a brief span of time. In his *Methodist Adventures in Negro Education*, J. S. Stowell (pp. 34-35) wrote the following:

On Christmas Day of the year 1865, Bishop E. Thompson presided at the meeting of the Negro ministers held in Wesley Chapel, New Orleans, at which the Mississippi Mission Conference, one of the first Colored Conferences in the Methodist Episcopal Church, was organized. There were present at this meeting, men from Mississippi, Louisiana, Alabama, and Texas. At an appropriate time in the proceedings the Bishop said, "And now brothers, you must elect one of your number as secretary."

This caused some stir among the Colored brothers, and at last one of them was obliged to explain to the Bishop that, while several of those present had been able to read a little, there was no one of them who could write. A white man was found to fill the position.

In 1883, however, just 18 years later, the curriculum of Gammon Theological School included Hebrew and Greek in its first-year course of study for students. Some of these early graduates were good students, and became remarkable leaders in the church.

Gammon, across the years, has been the center for many training programs such as seminars for district superintendents, conferences on ministerial training for the boards of ministry of the 19 black annual conferences, Christian education institutes, and other activities. It served as headquarters for the correspondence school for pastors who could not attend the seminary. Included in my duties was that of director of the correspondence school. Other members of the faculty participated.

One cannot fully appreciate the progress that has been made in race relations if one did not live through some of those early days. I recall, for example, that in 1946, President Henry Pitt Van Dusen, of Union Theological Seminary, and a former teacher of mine, was scheduled to give a series of lectures at the Candler School of Theology, Atlanta. I had been greatly impressed by him as a student, and was eager for some of students at Gammon to hear this most distinguished theologian, but it was not the practice for blacks to attend meetings at Candler. I questioned this practice to one of my colleagues in Christian education at Candler, Professor Emmett Johnson. He and I worked together on various boards and projects in the city, and I had found him to be one of the finest spirits in the church. He conferred with a few people at the university. The decision was to extend to us an invitation. He and a group of Candler students, equal in number to those who would come from Gammon, would meet us at the chapel door, escort us in, and sit with us.

The Gammon students resisted the plan initially, but I convinced them that we should go. It would be good for Candler as well as for us. The silly barriers had to be broken at some time and at some point. The truly brave folks were Professor Johnson and the students who dared to associate themselves with him that fateful evening. Interestingly enough, it was the beginning of the end of the practice of excluding blacks from the university campus. When we entered, a few of the students gave disapproving glances, but our presence was accepted without incidence. What a sad commentary it was that such a practice ever existed. It shows also how far the church has come since those days.

There was a long tradition of interracial meetings on the Gammon campus, and some of the white students would attend. But the Gammon students had come to feel that they had reached a dead end if some of the meetings could not be held on the white college campuses. The mood of the times, however, was not conducive to interracial meetings.

X

The Issue of Race

My own convictions have always been that the ultimate solution of the American race problem can never be found in separatism. We can never afford to yield to it, however difficult, and sometimes discouraging, the road to an inclusive society might appear. With this point of view, experiences that would otherwise appear humiliating, are seen as the reflections of the sickness of our society, and the depth of understanding and forthrightness needed to cope with it.

One could relate countless illustrations. I recall, for example, attending a meeting sponsored by the Division of the Local Church at the Cincinnati Club, in the middle forties. I was given a room there, but when I accompanied the other members of the group (all white) to the dining room for lunch, I was refused admission. When some of the members of the group protested, they were told "We don't serve Negroes here." I could be included only if the group ate together in a private room. The immediate crisis was resolved when Dr. John Q. Schisler, executive secretary, had his lunch and mine sent up to his room. The other meals were served in a private room.

Nashville, Tennessee is headquarters for three of the general boards of the church—General Board of Education, Board of Discipleship, and the United Methodist Publishing House. Blacks were not allowed in hotels for whites, and the public facility for blacks was a dingy rooming house with inadequate equipment and no place to eat. Since this was the general pattern of southern society, the plight of the blacks was merely taken for granted. The few who cared could do nothing about it.

Through the constant agitation of the blacks, and an increasing number of whites, the church later devised a policy to not hold its meetings at any place where blacks were discriminated against.

The following resolution was adopted by the General Conference of 1932:

That the General Conference of the Methodist Episcopal Church shall hereafter meet only in cities where hotels, sufficient in number to accommodate its delegates, shall in writing agree to meet the following conditions:
(1) No segregation of specific groups in room assignments.
(2) No discrimination against any delegates in the use of hotel services or entrances, lobbies, elevators, dining room and other facilities.
(3) Specific instructions of hotel employees by the hotel authorities regarding the interracial character of the Conference and the treatment of all delegates with equal courtesy.
(General Conference Journal, 1932, p. 832 cf.) Blacks were not treated well in Atlantic City where the 1932 Conference was held.

Although the resolution was passed it was not readily adopted in 1932, and efforts were made to table it. It is ironic that the Methodist Episcopal Church lost sight of this commitment, particularly in the adoption of a segregated stance in the merged church.

In fairness, it should be said that while a number of places around the country received interracial groups they, at best, merely endured them. A friend of mine told me of a meeting he attended where he and a number of black delegates were sitting in the hotel lounge following the dinner meal. One of the white bishops called him aside and said, "We would have far fewer problems with you fellows staying here if you didn't make yourselves so visible. Why don't you go up to your rooms?"

The friend retorted, "Are you telling me to go up to my room and hide because I'm black?"

This is as far as the nation, and certainly the church, had come in the forties. We must see where we were in order to measure the distance we have come, as well as the long distance which lies ahead.

The blacks in the Methodist Episcopal Church were often ridiculed by members of the black Methodist denominations, as being members of a segregated church. They were accused of lacking initiative, independence, and self-reliance. The blacks themselves felt segregated and subordinated. They were organized into black annual conferences, and until 1920 white bishops presided over them. For all practical purposes, on the local church and annual conference levels, it was almost the same as a separate denomination.

The white bishops had special blacks in each annual conference, who were their informers and advisors. The advisor may have been a district superintendent, or he may not have had any official connection with the cabinet at all. I could give instances of more than one white bishop who would have his informer meet him at the railroad station when he was passing through the city on the train on the way to another destination. Usually, the informer had written to the bishop giving him reports on the men and the churches, and the conference was to discuss the report. Almost all passenger trains carried mail and baggage, so in a city of any considerable size, the train waited thirty minutes or more for the unloading and loading of baggage and mail. In the South, there were always two waiting rooms—one read For Whites and the other For Colored.

Blacks could not enter the white waiting room except as servants, but a white man could come into the colored waiting room and hold a conference with a black man, without interference. This the bishop would do. When the conference was over, the bishop would return to his plush bedroom in the pullman car. His informer would go back to his segregated brethren, to report to them under the veil of secrecy whatever promises he had secured for the selected few—his supporters in the annual conference. It was a vicious system; although the bishop did not intend for that to be the case, it usually worked out that way. If one wanted to get ahead in the conference, he had to be in the good graces of the informer, for he was the man who had the bishop's ear, so to speak. This had all sorts of political ramifications. The informer usually led the delegation to the General Conference and to other important gatherings.

This happened, not because the white bishops were unsympathetic—some of them were genuinely concerned; but their contact with the blacks, except in very special instances, was indirect, and they felt safer relying on the judgment of persons whom they assumed were the conference leaders.

The mission of the church was largely a mission to the Negro, rather than a mission with the Negro. Whatever may have been the justification of some of it, it was, by and large, a separated ministry rather than a community of believers. It was what the church did for the blacks; not what the whites and blacks did together.

The tasks of Bishop Robert E. Jones and Bishop Matthew W. Clair, Sr., elected as general superintendents in 1920 (the first blacks ever elected), were not easy ones. While the blacks were more than proud to have two from their group elected to this high office, the preachers were not always happy over the exacting discipline these bishops required. Their work was entirely among the black conferences. They learned to know the preachers better, and insisted on a higher lever of performance than the white bishops usually did.

The black bishops suffered a great disadvantage in the work load they carried. Bishop Jones was assigned to the New Orleans area, which covered Louisiana, Mississippi, and Texas. Of course, Bishop Clair was assigned to Liberia for his first quadrennium; the second quadrennium he was given the Covington area, with general oversight of Liberia.

There is an interesting story about why the residence (headquarters of the bishop) for Bishop Clair was placed in Covington, Kentucky, instead of Cincinnati, Ohio, which would have been much better for transportation purposes. The reason is said to have been that the white bishop's residence was in Cincinnati, and the church could not afford to have two resident bishops in the same city. This unwritten rule did not prevail following the inauguration of the jurisdictional system. More will be said about that later.

The question might be raised, Why *did* the blacks stay with the Methodist Episcopal Church under the many pressures and indirections? Among the reasons, as I see them, were:

1. The blacks dared to feel a part of the whole church, whatever its shortcomings might have been. They could do more working from the inside than they could by leaving the church where they would not have any basis for an impact.

2. The Methodist Episcopal Church had been supportive of the blacks in the Emancipation movement.

3. Following the Emancipation, the church turned its attention to the education of black people—built schools, came as teachers, and showed concern for their general welfare.

4. Although with some dissatisfaction at times, it had shepherded the leadership of the black churches, and constantly sought to improve it. It sent teachers and missionaries.

5. It had never completely deserted the blacks. Among the whites in the church, there were always spokesmen for the cause of the blacks.

6. The blacks could make their own voices heard through their delegates who were members of general church bodies. They always had a court of appeals within the church that they would not have outside it.

7. It had helped to keep the hopes of the blacks alive—the hope of a better life here as well as hereafter.

8. However difficult it seemed to achieve, the blacks believed (and still do) that the inclusive church is the Church of Christ and they wanted to be members of Christ's Church.

The blacks' continued presence in the Methodist Church has served, to some extent, as a reminder that in the Church of Christ there is "neither Greek nor Jew, slave nor free, male nor female, but we are all one in Christ."

XI

Life as Editor

In 1948, John Wesley E. Bowen, editor of the *Central Christian Advocate,* was elected a bishop, and I was elected as his successor. The *Advocate,* under various names, existed from 1866 to 1966. Its first official editor was Dr. Joseph C. Hartzell (white), later Bishop Hartzell. This paper was published officially for the black annual conferences, although it was widely read throughout the church. While the caption it carried for many years, "The Voice of Methodism," could hardly be justified, since the General Conference is the only agency that can claim that title, the message it carried for many years made a great impact on its readers. Its comments on important church issues were the only ones many of its readers ever received. The paper helped to keep them in touch with the general church, since their personal contacts with the general church and many of the issues involved were so limited.

In the early days, it carried such items as the exposition of the weekly Sunday school lessons, and many of the Sunday school teachers drew on this source for help. It was through this paper that the blacks could make their voices heard on the various issues confronting them and the church. It was one of the few papers in the church where a black picture was carried with pride. I can remember when the *Christian Advocate* (The general Advocate for the church) carried the picture of a black chaplain during World War II. Dr. Roy L. Smith, who was editor of the *Christian Advocate,* told me that several thousand subscriptions were cancelled on that account. So there was a profound need for the *Central Christian Advocate.*

Practically all the editors of the *Central Christian Advocate,* before my time, were elected to the episcopacy. The editorship was considered a most important and influential position, and the editors were usually chosen with great care. The job also gave its holder wide visibility—his name and editorials were before the church each week, and he usually visited all the annual conferences, and was given a chance to address them, so it was natural for him to be given serious consideration when episcopal elections took place.

By the time I came along, it was the sentiment of a small group that a layman, who could not become a bishop, should be elected editor. A distinguished layman wrote an article to that effect and it was carried in the *Advocate.*

The headquarters of the paper was in New Orleans, Louisiana. Soon after my arrival the lay leader of the New Orleans district came to my office and invited me to be the speaker for their annual meeting. I consented to do it. He then leaned over and said, just above a whisper, "I am so happy you can come. You see, the last thing we want is to have a preacher speaking to us."

I had to tell him that my classification was clergy, and gave him the chance to withdraw the invitation.

He said, "No, you are not a regular preacher; you are more like one of us."

While I knew he was just trying to wriggle his way out of an embarrassing situation, I accepted his words as a goal toward which to strive as an editor—to always be close enough to the laity in the editorship of the paper so there would be a feeling of oneness among us. I purposed to make them feel that the paper spoke to them and for them; that it spoke to the church, and in a measure, for the church, and that it always embraced the Christian interpretation of life.

This had been the nature of the *Advocate,* historically, and perhaps the reason the lay leader accepted me on face value as "one of us."

I came to the editorship of the *Advocate* at a most crucial moment in the history of the church. There is a sense, of course, in which every moment is crucial and presents its own set of demands. In 1948, the jurisdictional system was eight years old. The Central Jurisdiction had been merely tolerated by the blacks, as a whole, but never really accepted. There were some members who were willing to exploit it for the leadership advantages they felt it offered. Some looked at it despairingly; while others looked at it as a way station to a more perfect union.

During the depression, the church found it necessary to curtail expenses at every point, and the *Southwestern Christian Advocate,* as it was called then, was struggling for survival. One technique of helping it along was to pull feature articles from the *Christian Advocate* as a filler, and leave space for editorials and news items from the local churches, also matters of general interest to the blacks alone. This practice began around 1932. While the change was a disappointment to many of the blacks, it was tolerated as a means of saving the paper. The price of subscriptions did not cover publication costs, and the jurisdictional system had not as yet been conceived. The blacks still took pride in this historic publication and generally rallied to support it.

With the coming of the jurisdictional system in 1939, the blacks became increasingly restive for having to be in a separate jurisdiction. They also strongly disliked having material—frequently irrelevant and sometimes offensive—imposed on them, which had been prepared exclusively for the five white jurisdictions. When I was elected editor in 1948, this practice had moved beyond the level of tolerance and something had to be done. The argument that the paper operated at a deficit was unimpressive. The more radical group insisted that a church which could afford to separate its members into white and black could afford to provide for the blacks a paper through which they could express their hopes and aspirations.

The Board of Publication agreed to make such a paper possible. The old practice was abandoned, the format was changed, the paper became a biweekly instead of a weekly publication, and the pages were increased from 16 to 24.

There were those who applauded the change; while others saw little significance in it. There was still the segregated jurisdiction, and although the paper had changed its face, some felt it was little more than an expression of the system. The principle of "separate but equal" was soon to be declared unconstitutional by the Supreme Court of the United States. The blacks had long known the principle to be a myth, but a large majority of the jurisdictional members saw a purpose in the paper, and gave it their support.

The task of the editor was not a simple one. While the *Discipline* defined his job to be that of editing the paper, circulation was as much his responsibility as editing. It was not planned that way, but that is how it worked out. The responsibility for publishing and circulating the paper was in the hands of the publishers. What complicated the matter was that the circulation manager was dirctly responsible to the publishers, who were in Nashville, Tennessee, and they were far too busy to give serious consideration to the circulation of the *Central Christian Advocate*, whose circulation manager was in New Orleans. There were times when coordination became extremely difficult, but the paper managed to survive.

In my attempt to lift the journalistic level of the paper, I found it necessary to abridge, and at times curtail, many reports from local churches about things like chicken suppers, or some preacher who preached an inspiring sermon. This made a lot of local church news reporters quite unhappy. In an effort to explain what makes news, I said to a group, "Just to say the minister preached a inspiring sermon is not news." One lady replied, "In my church it is. It so seldom happens."

With the new format, there was much more work to do. Feature articles had to be written, and pictures secured to illustrate them. I found it difficult to get writers and depend on their keeping a schedule. In addition to the editorials, there were times when I had to write the feature articles as well. I wrote them under pseudonyms so it would not look like a one-man paper, and sometimes so I might present another side of an issue.

The paper later attracted some excellent writers, however, who helped to keep the pertinent concerns of the readers in clear focus. It finally overcame this initial inertia and exercised an important function in the Central Jurisdiction.

While the *Central Christian Advocate* was published for the Central Jurisdiction, it was not always simple to determine the kind of paper it should be. The *Christian Advocate* was available to all persons who cared to subscribe to it, and some members of the central jurisdiction received it, although the vast majority did not. What would be the distinct role of the *Central Christian Advocate?* What kind of a paper would the jurisdiction subscribe to with any degree of enthusiasm? What kind of a paper would the Board of Publication support?

The merging of churches was still a relatively new thing, and North, South, and Methodist Protestant relationships were not strong—the issue of blacks in the church was a carefully guarded one. There was always the danger of triggering an explosion. These were the Joe McCarthy days, when an editor could be liquidated almost overnight if he could be accused of leaning toward the left. It was not easy for one to deal with any issue forthrightly without earning the reputation of being at least "pink." Yet, if one dared to give any significant editorial leadership, he or she had to take that risk.

I decided early to hold before me certain presuppositions and guidelines, and to follow them quite diligently, and I hope daringly. It was my conviction that the paper should always reflect a Christian perspective. Its tasks were to inform, interpret, inspire, and provoke thought and action. This approach would require an honest search for the facts before attempting an assessment of an issue; an analysis of the facts in such a way as to explore all the angles (there are no one-sided issues); presenting what seems to be the logical conclusion on the basis of the facts at hand; and suggesting a course of action, if the data justifies it.

It is said that a good doctor is one who can not only make the proper diagnosis, but who can also prescribe the medicine in such doses that the patient can keep it on his stomach. Someone put it another way, "Some people hit the nail on the head every time they strike, but they hit so hard that they bust the board." While there are times when people need to be jolted out of complacency and indifference, if not plain hostility, it should be done in such a way that the reactions will ultimately be positive rather than negative. I was convinced that the paper should be an arm of support for the community of believers in the Church of Christ. While no editor ever lives up to such a great demand, the goal should ever be before him. Whether the paper moved in that direction during my tenure of office must be left to the judgment of others.

XII

The Central Jurisdiction

Up to this point in my life, my main interests had been focused on my work of the time—student, pastor, teacher, editor, but now my increasingly wider participation in the life of the church gave me responsibility and concern for many more of its phases with which I shall deal separately.

The Central Jurisdiction remained one of the primary issues with which the church had to struggle. Because the Central Jurisdiction cut across the other five geographical jurisdictions, it was defined in terms of race. The legislation pertaining to it reads: "Central—The Negro Annual Conferences, Negro Mission Conferences and Missions in the United States of America" (*Discipline*, 1939, par. I, Article 26). One must also keep in mind that the Uniting Conference of 1939 made the boundaries of the respective jurisdictions a part of the constitution, and given the climate of the time, made it virtually impossible to change them.

The leaders of the Central Jurisdiction never accepted the jurisdictional arrangement as final, and worked from the beginning to ultimately eliminate it. It was in a large measure the concern of the Central Jurisdiction, which kept the problem constantly before the rest of the church.

James P. Brawley, then president of Clark College, Atlanta, at the Central Jurisdictional Conference, held at Clark, 1948, offered a resolution that the conference set up a commission to study the jurisdiction. The resolution was adopted and the bishops empowered to name the commission. A year passed and nothing was done. Dr. Brawley and Prince Taylor met with the College of Bishops in 1949 and urged the bishops to name the commission. The bishops named Dr. Brawley chairman and Prince Taylor was named secretary. While a number of people across the jurisdiction were placed on the commission, the jurisdictional conference did not make any financial provisions for the commission to do its work, so the work was done by those who could arrange their own travel. But it was the work of this commission that helped to influence the action of the General Conference in 1952, and all subsequent actions until the Central Jurisdiction was finally abolished.

In that memorable Episcopal Address of 1952, delivered by Bishop Paul Kern (memorable for both its quality and length), the bishops declared:

To discriminate against a person solely upon the basis of his race is both unfair and unchristian. Every child of God is entitled to that place in society which he has won by his industry and his character. To deny that position of honor because of the accident of his birth is neither democracy nor good religion (DCA, 1952).

It is significant to note that Bishop Kern was a former bishop of the Methodist Episcopal Church, South. He wrote the address, although it had to receive the approval of the other members of the Council of Bishops. To have a bishop of the South take such forthright leadership on the position of race at that time was noteworthy indeed.

This address formed the basis of a resolution adopted by the General Conference under the caption, "The Methodist Church and Race." It read in part:

The problem facing Methodism in the matter of race is perhaps the most crucial problem before our world today. Therefore it presents to us a God-given opportunity. In keeping, therefore, with the thrilling challenge set forth in the Episcopal Address, we purpose that the church seek to free itself utterly from racial discrimination and segregation.

To this end we recommend as specific and immediate steps:

1. That there be opportunity without discrimination or segregation for full participation in all the activities of the church by the many racial and national groups that make up our Methodist fellowship.

2. That there be equality of accommodations for all races at national and international meetings of the church.

3. That the institutions of the church, local churches, colleges, universities, theological schools, hospitals, and homes carefully restudy their policies and practices as they relate to race, making certain that these policies and practices are Christian.

4. In keeping with the rapid advance being made in the direction of widening employment on democratic principles, that the agencies and institutions of the Methodist Church employ their staffs on the basis of character and qualifications, without racial discrimination.

5. In view of the fact that the churches of the Central Jurisdiction may, in some cases, very properly desire to become a part of another Jurisdiction in which they are located, we call attention to the enabling legislation (par. 538, 1952 Discipline) making such readjustments easier of attainment (par. 2027, 1952 Resolution).

When I was a boy, the older people of the black community had an expression which aptly describes this kind of effort: "Such shuffling of the vessels for such little victuals."

But the action is not to be taken lightly, for cumbersome as it was, it was at least a "leak in the dike." At first it involved less than a dozen churches in places like Colorado, New York, and Pennsylvania. The South in 1952 felt greatly threatened to even anticipate a transfer of a local church happening anywhere, for to them the Central Jurisdiction was sealed at Union, never to be broken.

James P. Brawley, one of the architects of the dissolution of the Central Jurisdiction, points out in his *Two Centuries of Methodist Concern*, that the time was ripe for the movement toward integration. While his special reference was to the black college campuses primarily, it relates also to the movement of the church. He takes the position that the black student revolution was inevitable and gives three reasons for it.

1. The time was right and the climate ready for recognition of people as human beings with dignity and the right to freedom. . . .

The Universal Declaration of Human Rights in 1948 had created a world climate for rebellion against oppression, injustice, discrimination and humiliation of the darker peoples of the world. . . .

2. The courts had prepared the way in decisions bearing on segregation and gave encouragement to make the venture to change the hoary customs, though this was a daring and dangerous expedition.

3. The generations of the sixties were heirs of a heritage of culture and courage, accumulated over a period of a century through education in schools that had for their purpose the freeing of the mind and spirit of black people. . . .

The General Conference of 1952 dealt only with the transfer of a local church from one annual conference to another, which required the approval, not only of the two annual conferences, but also the two jurisdictional conferences involved and the final approval of the General Conference.

The 1956 General Conference dealt with the transfer of a local church, an annual conference from one jurisdiction to another, and a bishop of the Central Jurisdiction to another jurisdiction, and simplified the process. This was done by a constitutional amendment, known as Amendment IX.

The General Conference recognized the voluntary character of the amendment. It provided no deadlines; it merely established a plan for those churches and conferences that desired to move ahead. It did speak to the issue of the abolition of the Central Jurisdiction in the following manner:

The Central Jurisdiction shall be abolished when all of the annual conferences now comprising it have been transferred to other jurisdictions in accordance with the voluntary procedure of Article V. . . . Each remaining bishop of the Central Jurisdiction shall thereupon be transferred to the jurisdiction to which the majority of the membership of his area have been transferred, and the Central Jurisdiction shall then be dissolved.

The debates concerning the Central Jurisdiction were long, and at times, heated. Some people felt that the racially segregated jurisdiction damaged the image of the Methodist Church and the church needed to improve its image. In addition to Amendment IX, a number of proposals were suggested such as annexing the Central with Northeastern, North Central or Western jurisdictions. Others thought that the General Conference should just abolish the Central Jurisdiction and let the black conferences fall into the jurisdictions where they were geographically located. Without careful planning this approach would have been oversimplistic and irresponsible.

The Central Jurisdiction did not warm up to any of these approaches for at least two reasons. The first was because blacks wanted to be a part of the whole church, not just a part of a part of it. Second, the leaders of the jurisdiction realized that the Central Jurisdiction as a structure was merely a reflection of the problem, which ultimately was segregation in the Methodist Church. The jurisdiction could have been abolished, and the blacks found stranded on islands of segregation—hopeless, powerless, and defeated. All this fear was well-founded, for although segregation is a church-wide issue, it is also local, and if it persists on the local level, little is accomplished by eliminating its form on the national and international levels. It is where and how the people congregate that make or hinder community. Some felt that this superficial integration would be worse than no integration, for it would be deceiving in the first place, and second, it would be a form without any force.

The blacks were frequently made to feel uncomfortable by the characteristic approach that integration meant the surrender of black churches or schools to join with white groups. This approach invariably carried the implication that what was black was inherently inferior to what was white, and therefore not worth preserving.

Many Methodists knew that it was one thing to set up a formula by which the Central Jurisdiction might ultimately be liquidated, and a vastly different one to make it work. The Supreme Court decision on segregated public schools was handed down in 1954, but by 1960 little had been done to put it into action. There were those who had hoped that Amendment IX would suffer the same fate; but there were others who were determined that it would not. Consequently the ferment for the dissolution of the Central Jurisdiction continued.

As a result of the wide range of attitudes within the church, many resolutions concerning the Central Jurisdiction were sent to the General Conference of 1956. The Committee on Conferences, to which the General Conference referred these resolutions, found the task of handling them so delicate and complicated that it assigned this work to a special subcommittee composed of one person from each jurisdiction; Ralph W. Sockman, Northeastern Jurisdiction; Edwin L. Jones, Southeastern Jurisdiction; Charles Ray Goff, North Central Jurisdiction; John R. Wilkins, Western Jurisdiction; Robert E. Goodrich, South Central Jurisdiction; and Prince A. Taylor, Jr., Central Jurisdiction. This was not an easy assignment. Along with those persons in the General Conference who had honest differences of opinion, there were a few vocal mischief makers who conspired to capitalize on the issue in order to advance themselves politically. There were also those who felt that the jurisdictional representative should represent their special point of view rather than examine the issue with an open mind.

For some reason, which is not clear to me now, we did not meet in a private room, and a few of the politicians gathered around where we were meeting, close enough to monitor the conversations. The committee ignored them and went on with its work as though they were not there.

After meeting for several hours, the committee decided to recommend the organization of a study commission of seventy persons on which every jurisdiction would be adequately represented. Its work was defined as follows:

1. To make a thorough study of our jurisdictional system, with special reference to its philosophy, its effectiveness, its weaknesses, and its relationship to the future of the Methodist Church.

2. To carry on studies and conduct hearings in all the jurisdictions on racial segregation in the Methodist Church and all other problems related to the jurisdictional system.

3. To develop courses of action directed toward greater interracial brotherhood and the spirit of Christian love.

4. In the performance of its duties this commission shall draw upon other agencies of the Methodist Church to assist in such research.

5. To distribute to the churches such facts and information during the quadrennium as may be deemed helpful to the work of this commission and of value to the church.

6. To report its findings and recommendations to the General Conference of 1960. . . .

The question of who would form the commission became an issue. My own proposal was to let the Council of Bishops do it since the council was the most representative body in the church and knew the delegates fairly well. But there was opposition to the suggestion. One member of the committee was slightly anti-bishop and felt that the bishops should not be given this power. He wanted to tone down the bishops. Another member said he would like to be on the Commission of seventy, and if it were left to the bishops, his own bishop would not name him. Still another member felt that the selection of the commission should be more democratic and suggested involving the various delegations in the process. Another member felt that the bishops could not be trusted to include enough "go-slow" representatives on the commission. We finally got around to the following compromise which the Committee on Conferences approved and the General Conference adopted:

This Commission shall be composed of one minister and one lay person from each Jurisdiction for each 500,000 church members or major fraction thereof, with a minimum of three ministers and three lay persons from each Jurisdiction. Members of the Commission shall be elected by this General Conference upon nominations by the Council of Bishops after consultation between the Bishops and the Chairmen of the Annual Conference delegations within their respective jurisdictions. Officers of the Commission shall be elected by the Commission from the above named and elected members. The members shall also include twelve Bishops, two from each Jurisdiction, and twelve additional laymen, two from each Jurisdiction, nominated by the Council of Bishops and elected by the General Conference. . . .

The committee recommended that the Council of Bishops appoint a convener to convene the commission within six months following the General Conference.

Of course, Amendment IX had its problems too. It was not only a voluntary arrangement, but by the process of attrition it could weaken the part of the jurisdiction that remained, so that it would be difficult to do its work.

Efforts were made at the 1960 General Conference to fix a target date for the complete transfer of all the churches by 1968, but failed. (See DCA, 1360, pp. 177, 184.)

One of the last editorials I wrote in the *Central Christian Advocate*, published July 15, 1956 (one month after I was elected a bishop), was an effort to give some balance to the many kinds of resolutions that were being discussed for proposal at the next General Conference. The editorial, "Analyzing Proposals for Integration," sought to put into focus the fundamental issue—integration in the Methodist Church, of which the Central Jurisdiction was only a factor, although a very significant one. The editorial noted that it would be possible to do away with the Central Jurisdiction, or even the jurisdictional system, and still have segregation in the church. An inclusive fellowship would be the goal.

There had been interesting indications that interracial relations had begun to improve. In 1950, Bishop James C. Baker, of the Western Jurisdiction, invited Bishop Alexander P. Shaw, of the Central Jurisdiction, to preside over the Southern Arizona Annual Conference. This act was so singular that the national press gave it wide publicity. A special editorial was devoted to it in the *Central Christian*

Advocate (March 16, 1950). This same year, the students of the Candler School of Theology voted by an overwhelming majority to admit black students to the School of Theology.

On the other hand, the Georgia legislature voted for more than $90,000.00 for education, with two stern provisos. "First, if the white school, the University of Georgia, voluntarily admits a Negro, it will be cut off without a cent of state funds. Second, if any white school admits a Negro by court order, the whole public school or university (depending on which the order applies to) will be cut off" (CCA March 29, 1951, p. 2). The legislature had in mind the U.S. Supreme Court doctrine, "Where Negro education is separate, it must be equal to that of whites." This doctrine led, after court fights, to the admittance of blacks to white universities in Texas, Oklahoma, Kentucky, and other states.

The Commission of Seventy met and organized for its work. It elected Charles C. Parlin, Sr., distinguished lawyer and churchman as chairman. Dr. Parlin, a graduate of Harvard Law School, had already represented the Newark Annual Conference for six quadrennia, beginning as a lay delegate to the General Conference in 1940. He was vice president of the World Methodist Council, secretary of the Commission on Church Union, a member of the presidium of the World Council of Churches, and a member of the General Board of the National Council of Churches, as well as many other significant positions.

Dr. Parlin's breadth of mind, intimate knowledge of the church, global understanding and concern, and his innate sense of justice, eminently qualified him for this position. A person less sensitive and less understanding of the total situation could hardly have given the church this leadership in 1956.

The task of the commission was of such magnitude that it elected a full-time executive secretary to coordinate its work. The Reverend Dr. Cooper C. Bell, a ministerial member of the Virginia Annual Conference, Southeastern Jurisdiction; a Phi Beta Kappa; chairman of the Committee on Conferences at the 1956 General Conference; and a member of the Commission of Seventy, proved to be an excellent choice. In addition to his leadership qualifications, Dr. Bell had the advantage of being a southerner on the one hand, and a fair-minded person on the other. While the relationships at times became a bit uneasy, in general the South felt they could trust him, and the North and the Central jurisdictions felt they could work with him.

Of course, this "on the one hand" and "on the other" does not always satisfy everybody. The man who had committed a crime and was looking for a lawyer is a case in point. He deputized his friend to get him a good lawyer—a one-arm lawyer.

"Why a one-arm lawyer?" the friend asked.

"Because, when he argues my case, I don't want him talking about 'on the other hand.' "

Despite the vast differences of opinions inside the commission and throughout the church, the commission's study was a good one. In keeping with the mandate, it made its report to the 1960 General Conference. Charles Parlin presented it most astutely, giving a brief background of the issue of the blacks in the Methodist Church, analyzing the factors involved, and presenting the work and recommendations of the commission.

While the report was carefully presented, representing an enormous amount of work, it took up almost half of the total session of the General Conference. The commission had its problems also. The chairman reported that the commission had spent a total of twenty-two days during the quadrennium in discussions and debates on the respective issues. According to the report, they had held twenty-four hearings over the nation, and countless interviews.

There were persons who held extreme views, those who did not want to do anything, those who wanted to abolish the jurisdictional system, and those who wanted the total and immediate abolition of the Central Jurisdiction. There was also a considerable number of persons who wanted the abolition of the Central Jurisdiction only after careful study and plans had been made, but who felt that a fixed or target date should be set for the complete discontinuance of the Central Jurisdiction. The commission did not make this recommendation to the General Conference, although they had considered it at great length. The commission took the position that the target date of 1968 would be counter-productive, since Amendment IX stated that the process would be voluntary. The efforts made to have a fixed date did not prevail. This was one of the most sensitive points in the entire discussion, within the commission and the General Conference.

The chairman of the commission reported that the commission found strong opposition to the jurisdictional system in the Northeastern, North Central and Western jurisdictions and, to some extent, in the Central Jurisdiction. In the Southeastern and South Central jurisdictions, however, there was a strong desire to hold onto the jurisdictional system. (These two jurisdictions represented a minority in the church.) According to Dr. Parlin, there was the fear that the six jurisdictions, for all practical purposes, would end up in six different churches. This would lead to provincialism.

Although many of the issues remained unsettled, the time spent discussing them, by both the commission and the General Conference, was not wasted. It gave opportunity for an openness of expression and exposure to many points of view that the church had never faced before, and a better working relationship emerged. Some of the fears had been allayed, and the North, South, black and white were able to talk with one another with a little greater trust. The discussions revealed that an increasing number of delegates were developing an awareness that the Central Jurisdiction could no longer be thought of as a permanent solution to the problem of race in the Methodist Church. It seemed that the jurisdictional system had a much longer future.

It was the implementation of Amendment IX that appeared

to have been the real task of the church for the quadrennium 1960-64. The amendment was voluntary, of course, but there was the need for much encouragement on every level of church life to make it work. The Commission of Seventy recommended the establishment of an Interjurisdictional Relations Commission to consist of thirty-six persons for this purpose.

This commission was to examine the intricate problems involved and encourage the kind of interracial relationships which would develop attitudes conducive to mutual understanding and goodwill. The commission was instructed to make reports to the Council of Bishops, and to the church through the church press. It would make its final report to the General Conference of 1964.

The General Conference outlined specifically areas of consideration on local, district, annual conferences, and general church levels which the commission was to take into account (*Discipline*, 1960, paragraph 2013).

I was elected a bishop by the Central Jurisdictional Conference, which was held in New Orleans, June 16, 1956, and assigned to the Monrovia area, Liberia, West Africa. This assignment took me away from direct involvement in the work of integrating the jurisdictions until my return eight years later. Upon the death of Bishop Vernon C. Middleton in 1965, I took his place on the Interjurisdictional Commission and remained until the end of the quadrennium when the commission was officially dissolved.

The Interjurisdictional Commission brought in a program to make Amendment IX work. The task was found by the commission not to be a simple one, for the real job was to rid the church of segregation. The elimination of the Central Jurisdiction was the only possible machinery through which progress might be made in that direction.

There were unresolved problems that had not been handled, such as the overlapping of annual conferences across jurisdictional lines, and the question of pensions and salaries for the preachers who transferred. Would bishops be transferred to other jurisdictions on the basis of equality? In a system of voluntarism, what would happen if some conferences were not transferred? Would this irreducible minimum be frozen into a helpless state of existence? Amendment IX did not spell out answers to these delicate and significant questions. These were some of the concerns which were posed in the report of the commission or raised from the General Conference floor in 1964.

The Central Jurisdictional Conference had already appointed a commission to deal with some of these problems, particularly the realignment of annual conferences so that no one annual conference in the racially composed jurisdiction would overlap the geographical jurisdictions. This helped to make sense out of the transfers when the church was ready to move.

The Interjurisdictional Commission recommended to the General Conference of 1964 the establishment of a temporary fund to give assistance to those churches which transferred, for the first four years, where such help was needed; the transfer of preachers without reducing their status in the annual conference to which they would transfer; that members of the Central Jurisdiction would not have to give up their membership on any general boards and agencies on which they were serving; that conferences to which Central Jurisdictional pastors transfer equalize their pension programs so that these preachers would share equal pension for service; that the educational and other institutions in the Central Jurisdiction become the responsibility of the whole church. It proposed, also, that the bishops from the Central Jurisdiction who were transferred to other jurisdictions would not count against the quota for the respective jurisdictions, and it would balance out only as retirement and death made it possible.

The General Conference also provided, for the first time, a terminal date for the elimination of the Central Jurisdiction, which read as follows: "If by September 1, 1967, for any reason the Central Jurisdiction shall not have been dissolved by the procedure of Amendment IX (#47 ix) the commission shall draft a plan for its termination to report to the General Conference of 1968."

By this time it was clear in the minds of most church leaders that the Central Jurisdiction had had its day and must now move into the larger church, but it was through the work of Charles Parlin that the movement went faster than was anticipated. In 1964 the Central Jurisdictional Conference was held one week before the conference of the Northeastern Jurisdiction. After my return from Liberia I was assigned by the Central Jurisdiction to what was then the Baltimore area, which consisted of the Washington and Delaware conferences, with residence in Baltimore, Maryland. Charles Parlin visited our conference and knew of my assignment.

Before the adjournment of the conference, I received a telephone call from W. Ralph Ward, host bishop for the Northeastern Jurisdictional Conference, inviting Belle and me to be guests of the jurisdiction. We went the next week to Syracuse, New York, the seat of the conference.

On our arrival, Charles came over to tell me that all of the legal requirements had been met for the transfer of the Baltimore area to the Northeastern Jurisdiction. The only requirement that remained was the certification from the College of Bishops of the Central Jurisdiction that the annual conferences had approved the transfer—staying within the boundaries of Amendment IX. If that could be secured, we could be transferred into the Northeastern Jurisdiction the next morning. I immediately contacted my colleagues and had each one certify, by telegram, that the amendment had been approved. The report was made the next morning and we were transferred in. It was the first area of the Central Jurisdiction to be transferred to a geographical jurisdiction and I was the first bishop. The Lexington area was transferred into the North Central about two weeks later, when their jurisdictional conference was held. Bishop James S. Thomas became the second bishop to be transferred.

Many of the details had not been worked out, and I knew

it, but I felt that the time had come to take the leap of faith.
The transfer created problems which no one had had time to
consider. Where would I be assigned? What would happen to
the two conferences to which I was originally assigned?
Should I be given another area? If I were to continue with two
conferences in the new jurisdiction, would not the act be
considered the transfer of segregation to another jurisdiction? Would not the abrupt dissolution of the conferences
without careful planning really be a setback to the blacks in
the new situation? Amendment IX merely called for the
transfer of churches and conferences; it did not provide for
the elimination of black conferences, once they were
transferred. The church had not been ready for that step in
1956 when the amendment was passed.

Added to the predicament was the fact that Bishop Newell
Booth, a member of the Northeastern Jurisdiction who had
been serving in Central Africa, was returning for residency in
his own jurisdiction. This meant that the conference had to
make provisions for the placement of two additional bishops,
and the creation of two additional episcopal areas, unless the
two conferences from the Central Jurisdiction were to be held
as a segregated area. This possibility was never given serious
consideration, although it was suggested by a few. After
considerable discussion and debate by the Episcopal Committee the new areas were finally fixed. They were the
Harrisburg area, formerly part of the Philadelphia area, and
the New Jersey area—the two New Jersey annual conferences; the Newark Conference (now northern New Jersey)
which was part of the New York area, and the New Jersey
Conference (now southern New Jersey) which had been a
part of the Philadelphia area.

I was given the New Jersey area, but there was still a
delicate problem the jurisdiction had to face—What would
happen to the two black conferences? Preparation had not
been made for their merger into the other conferences of the
Northeastern Jurisdiction in an orderly and satisfactory way.
The transfers came even faster than Charles Parlin, chairman

of the Interjurisdictional Commission, ever anticipated. In making his report to the Jurisdictional Conference, he apologized for not having it written and organized, but said that things had happened so fast that he did not have time to do it.

The matter of pensions, minimum salaries, the appointment of the twelve black district superintendents, and other pressing problems had to be resolved. The ultimate solution was to continue the two conferences for another year, under the supervision of Bishop John Wesley Lord of the Washington area, in whose geographical territory many of the black churches were located. This proved to be a wise solution, for under his capable leadership the details were worked out and in 1965 the churches were transferred to the annual conferences in which they were geographically located.

An early proposal was that I supervise these conferences and guide them through this period, but this would have been far too much of an administrative load.

The General Conference of 1964 granted Liberia Central Conference status, making it possible for them to elect their own bishop, but that would not be done until a year later. Upon the request of Liberia, the Council of Bishops had already assigned me to supervise the work there until such time as Liberia could elect its own bishop. This was in addition to the work of the New Jersey area.

Things were happening fast during those days. At the meeting of the Council of Bishops, held in Pittsburg, prior to the General Conference of 1964, the council decided that the time had come to elect a black bishop as president of the council. Although I had been in Liberia for eight years, I was elected president on the first ballot to take office the following year. This was the first time in the history of Methodism a black bishop was elected to the presidency of the council. I was greatly humbled by the generosity of my colleagues.

This act was so singular that it made headlines internationally. A photographer from *Time* magazine came to my office and took fifty pictures of me and selected the worst of the lot for publication. I thought about suing them, but they saved themselves from that by putting the name of Bishop James S. Thomas under my picture. Why he didn't sue, I don't know.

I remember so distinctly an interview I had with the press when I was first elected. One reporter asked me, "How does it feel to be the first Negro to be elected President of the Council of Bishops?"

My reply was, "If I find out that I was elected merely because I am a Negro I will resign. I am proud of my colleagues, that despite the old patterns, they did not allow my color to hinder my election."

I have never accepted that election in any personal way. To me, it was an expression by the Council of Bishops that if the church were to take integration seriously, the council should lead the way. It demonstrated the fact that the church had come of age. It was an expression of readiness of the council to take a significant step in removing racial barriers and boundaries in ways it had not done before.

Soon after I had been elected a bishop in 1954, one of my black colleagues in the council said to me: "Now, Prince, we bishops of the Central Jurisdiction don't try to speak on issues in the Council that do not pertain to our work in the Central Jurisdiction. We let them (speaking of the white bishops) fight out these other matters." I thought that to be rather strange, for I could think of no issue which affected the church at any point that was not the business of the council as a whole. Although I did not argue with my distinguished mentor, I knew that would not be my style of operation.

One had to live in those days to understand why the black bishops took such a stance. The merging of churches was not too far in the past, and the northern and southern bishops saw many issues differently. They had not fully learned to live together as a single body. When tension rose between the two groups, the black bishops did not want to be caught in the middle of it. They saw nothing to gain, and did not want to be used as scapegoats. Then too, the Central Jurisdiction was set apart as a racial unit and its leaders had to spend full time keeping the jurisdiction's problems, needs, and hopes before the church, and the bishops did not want to be sidetracked in this endeavor. The time had not come when the church was willing to accept the black bishops as representatives of the whole church. They would be heard on matters pertaining to the Central Jurisdiction, but were not expected to contribute to the solution of the larger problems of the church, except where they had special bearing on the blacks of the church. Theoretically, the black bishops had every right the white bishops had in the council, but this did not prevail in practice. Prior to 1960, no black bishop chaired a general board or agency in the church. Black staff members of boards and agencies, even when they were named as general staff people, were assigned to work in and with the Central Jurisdiction. Most of the assignments, however, were to departments of Negro work within the boards and agencies. These arrangements preconditioned the blacks to think in terms of their own destiny. So the bishops in the council concerned themselves with the issues of the blacks, although they were keenly aware of the work of the church as a whole.

The sixties was a period of considerable turmoil, when the blacks of the United States made definite gains—at least some of them did. But the sixties did not prepare the blacks in large numbers for integration. It aroused in them black awareness and black pride. They were taught to be proud of their color—black is beautiful. Before the sixties, many saw being black as a handicap, since they were treated as inferiors on the basis of their color. The intrigues of slavery and its aftermath stimulated separatism between blacks and whites, and between blacks and blacks. It created the condition for hostility of whites toward blacks, and disunity, distrust, and the lack of esteem among blacks. The Civil Rights Movement sought to free the blacks to be themselves, and instead of trying to move away from the characteristics of blackness, they accented them through dress, hairstyle, etc.

While the blacks may have at times overemphasized blackness, one has to understand the factors which forced them into it. They discovered that only as a group and through group action could they make gains, and be free persons in a free society. Although much of their apparent cohesiveness was more form than fact, they developed a kind of racial protectionism which tended to isolate them from the main stream. In this way, they were giving support to those in our society who seek to keep the races separate and the blacks disadvantaged.

My unalterable position is that separatism, voluntary or enforced, church or state, is contrary to the basic principles of justice and equality, and the tenets of the Christian faith, and can ultimately lead to the deterioration of our whole society. While I wholeheartedly support programs geared to strengthening ethnic minorities and all people who are victimized by social neglect, special care must be given so those programs will be means of bringing all people into common participation in the total life of the country. The goal should never be the forming of stronger blocks or segments—barriers rather than bridges to the integrated life. It should lead toward a more inclusive society and a common destiny. The United States is becoming, more and more, a nation of separated groups instead of a melting pot.

We can never take comfort in a pluralistic society that is more plural and fragmented than a community with diversity. Any pluralism defined and marked by racial demarcations, sets up boundaries that are ultimately self-defeating.

It may be noted that little has been said in this book about the significant union of the Evangelical United Brethren and the Methodist Church. The former EUBs gave important dimensions to the new church. My reason for not dealing with it is that it did not bring into the union the kind of sociological problems with which I have been basically dealing. The members of that tradition, on the whole, have stood for the inclusive church, and have given spiritual vitality to its life and work.

XIII

The Liberian Venture

In order for one to understand the setting in which the Liberian Church operated, something should be said about how the country became a nation. Liberia was the result of a project by a group of persons who in 1816 organized the American Colonization Society, for the purpose of settling freed blacks in Africa. It was a counterpart of a similar project which had already been carried out by the British in the settlement of such a group in Sierra Leone, beginning in the latter part of the 18th century.

The American Colonization Society was set up as a voluntary association formed for benevolent purposes. It was national in scope and character. Every American citizen contributing a fixed fee was eligible for membership. The first president of the society, Judge Bushrod Washington, was a nephew of President George Washington. Henry Clay was a prominent member and later, president; among other members were John Randolph and Francis Scott Key.

There is little doubt that the predominant motive for setting up the organization was the desire to rid the country of what was regarded as an alien group which many felt could never be integrated into the life of the country, and was becoming a source of difficulty. It was the hope of the society that the settlement of these people in a colony on the west coast of Africa might ultimately prove to be a happy solution to the situation of the blacks in the USA, and give them an opportunity to develop a homeland for themselves.

The view that the free blacks had no place in the American polity was not passively accepted. On January 16, 1817, a group of blacks released the following statement:

Our ancestors were, though not from choice, the first cultivators of the wilds of America, and we, their descendents, claim a right to share in the blessings of her luxuriant soil which their blood and sweat manured. We read with deep abhorrence the unmerited stigma, attempted to be cast on the free people of color that "they are a dangerous and useless part of the community." We declare that we shall be never separated from the slave population of this country: that to thrust the free people of color into the wilds of Africa without any sciences, and without a government of any kind, is to send them into perpetual bondage.
(A statement of a group of free Negroes in Philadelphia to Joseph Hopkinson, their representative in Congress—.)
The New Liberia, Lawrence A. Marinelli, p. 31.

But the group was not strongly supported and the movement continued.

Space will not allow for a detailed discussion of the society and its work, and it is not the purpose of this book to go into it. It is sufficient to note that the first settlers arrived on Providence Island in January, 1822 to begin a new life.

The story of how Liberia survived, developed, and became an independent nation in 1847 is one of the most intriguing stories in history. When a reporter in relatively recent years asked a Liberian diplomat why Liberia, the oldest republic in Africa, had not made the economic strides of some of the much younger nations, he said that Liberia had not had the advantages of colonialism. He was greatly criticized for the statement, mainly I think, because they did not understand what he meant, and he said it at a time when anti-colonialism was so strong that things were being interpreted emotionally.

While the European powers were investing funds and technology in their colonies for their own advantage, they also developed roads, ports, and institutions, and made available other resources that were not open to Liberia—The

Lone Star State. For all practical purposes, Liberia had to make it alone. Although Liberia became a sovereign state in 1847, the United States did not recognize her statehood until 1862. Britain recognized the country in 1848. It is generally conceded that our recognition was postponed because many members of Congress were not ready to recognize former slaves on any basis of equality. The signing of the Emancipation Proclamation by Abraham Lincoln made this feat possible.

While the lone star in the national flag symbolized the lone black repubic in Africa, it could have equally meant a lone and lonely nation struggling to survive. But history was on the side of Liberia, and her survival is a noteworthy achievement.

Despite the circumstances, Liberia has played a significant role in the independence movement in Africa, and is a stabilizing influence on the continent. She was a charter member of the United Nations, espoused the cause of black Africa, and kept alive the aspirations of independence. Nathan Barnes, Liberian Ambassador to the United Nations, the first black member of the Security Council, was president when Dag Hammarskjold was killed, and guided the council in the election of U Thant. During the 16th General Assembly, Miss Angie Brooks helped to make the transition of African states more peaceful than anyone would have imagined, and won for herself the title of The First Lady of African Independence.

Liberia played an important role in the peace-keeping efforts of the United Nations in the Congo, and her soldiers rendered valiant service there.

Under the presidency of William V. S. Tubman, Liberia was the leader in cooperative movements—the Sanniquellie Conference (Liberia) in 1959; the Monrovia Conference, 1961; the Lagos, Nigeria Conference, 1962; and the Addis Ababa, Ethiopia Conference, 1963. Her contribution in advice and counsel has been immeasureable.

It should be mentioned in passing that, although Liberia

has been greatly neglected by the United States, she remains America's closest African friend.

It is against this background that the early missionary enterprises in Liberia can be best understood. Unlike most of the efforts of the church beyond the borders of the United States, the work was not begun primarily for the natives of the country, but was an effort to minister to the needs of the transplanted people from the United States. The leaders of the colonization movement sensed the value of religion as a stabilizing force among the new settlers, and urged the churches to cooperate with their movement by sending missionaries to Liberia. Of course, the majority of the colonists had already formed religious attachments when they came to the new country. One of the first institutions to be set up in any new settlement was a house of worship. The colonists tended to follow the denominational pattern which they had accepted in the United States. In every community there was to be Methodist church and a Baptist church, the two denominations to which most of the settlers belonged.

It is important to recognize that the work was begun by the colonists under a leadership that had little technical training, with limited funds to carry on a worthwhile program. When the missionaries arrived they found a struggling church, and their problem was to try to regularize its doctrines and activities, and relate it to the larger institution in the United States. The Liberia Annual Conference of the Methodist Church was organized in 1834, twelve years after the first settlers arrived.

Before 1832 the Methodist Episcopal Church had not sent any missionaries overseas. The General Conference of 1824, acting on a resolution of the Missionary Society, passed the following resolution: "That it is expedient, whenever the funds of the Missionary Society will justify the measure, for the Episcopacy to select a missionary or missionaries to the Colony in Africa now established under the auspices of the American Colonization Society." Action was postponed for another 8 years. On May 7, 1832, Melville B. Cox was appointed.

Cox, a native of Maine, sailed from Norfolk, Virginia on the steamship *Jupiter*, November 6, 1832, and arrived in Monrovia, March 8, 1833. He began his work with great zeal and enthusiasm, like a man with a mission. His work was monumental in the sense that he carried with him an uncommon devotion to a cause the church considered a side issue at best. He was not a well man, said to have been tubercular. He would never have qualified under the rigid standards of the Board of Global Missions today. It was not long before he was stricken with the dreaded African fever (malaria), and died five months after his arrival.

Anticipating, no doubt, his early death, he said to a friend, "If I die in Africa you must come over and write my epitaph." When asked what it should be, Cox replied, "Though a thousand fall, let not Africa be given up." These words stood in bold relief in the recruitment of missionaries for Liberia.

A few missionaries trickled in and out of Liberia until 1844, when the effort was practically given up, largely due to health conditions. Africa became known as the white man's grave. Though the period was brief, some extraordinary people gave their lives to the service. Their devotion is remembered in Liberia with deep gratitude.

It has been mentioned earlier that Liberia differed somewhat from other places where missionaries were sent, in that the work was begun by the Liberians themselves and not the missionaries. The church was eleven years old when the missionaries came. In making claims of being the first, the Baptists said they organized the church as soon as the ship arrived; the Methodists said they organized on the ship. While these claims are without solid documentation, there are indications that the establishment of houses of worship was one of the first preoccupations of the early settlers.

While in most cases there was mutuality among them, the mission work and the church held a dichotomous relationship for all practical purposes. They coexisted. Although some missionaries were Annual Conference members, only a few had any significant impact on the local church. They worked in schools, hospitals, and other service agencies on missionary stations.

XIV

The Liberian Predicament

It should be noted that the missionary or missionaries, to be named by the episcopacy, were to be sent to the colony in Africa, which was established by the American Colonization Society. While the mandate did not exclude the other inhabitants, it did not have them in mind. The missionaries were sent to the colony. This narrow interpretation of missions was an unfortunate circumstance.

True enough, the missionaries themselves reached out into the hinterland in later years and extended the mission of the church. One might observe, of course, that the delay of eight years in implementing the resolution of the General Conference seems to indicate that Liberia was not a serious consideration of the (then) Methodist Episcopal Church.

It is my considered opinion that the attitude of the church reflected somewhat the attitude of the state concerning the people of Liberia, and that they have been considered step-children at best. The church came with too little too late. So did the state.

Many thoughts have run through my mind since the coup in Liberia, April 12, 1980. While one can only surmise, the question has to be raised as to whether or not the outcome of the country would have been different had both church and state (USA) shown greater concern for the welfare of all its people from the beginning of the colony's existence. At this point one can only make conjectures, but the issue is worth taking into account. Where Liberia will go from here is difficult to perceive. There is no doubt that the country has been set back for many years, and has lost many of the gains she made. A nation trying to work its way out of revolution has a long and treacherous path to tread. Whether or not the revolution would have been averted, or at least postponed, or taken a different form under a less exacting national leader is mere conjecture. There were, apparently, certain contributing factors President Tolbert's administration gave to the revolution.

XV

Our Years in Liberia

The assignment to Liberia was an interesting sequence in my family history. During the days of slavery my grandmother, Annie, and her brother, George, were scheduled to be sent to Liberia as teachers. They were prevented from making this plan a reality when Mississippi made the freeing of slaves illegal. When my wife, Annie Belle, was a student at Clark College she became interested in going to Liberia as a missionary and took courses at the School of Missions, Gammon Theological Seminary, in preparation for the work. Subsequent events turned the course of her life in another direction. Although I had no particular role in my assignment in 1956, it was one that Annie Belle and I received with glad hearts and with the feeling that God had a hand in it. It was the opening of a new door of opportunity, education, and challenge for us, and it was not long before we discovered that it was indeed a different and exciting world.

Our leaving the country of our birth had brought complications, however. Our only daughter, Isabella, was in graduate school at Columbia University. She was younger than the usual university student, and our family ties were very close. Following her graduation in the spring, she would be employed by Catholic Charities, New York City, as a reading therapist, and we would be four thousand miles away. We did have the satisfaction of knowing that her Aunt Alberta (Belle's sister) and her husband lived in New York, and they loved Isabella as though she were their own child.

I can never forget our farewell at the Idlewild (now Kennedy) Airport. She appeared so brave as we were leaving. As the plane pulled off we watched out of the window for the last wave of her hand. When she was out of sight, we sat in silence for a few minutes, but each knew what was going on in the other's mind and heart. We shortly became adjusted and turned our thought toward the land which would be our new home and responsibility.

Liberia had been considered a hardship area for many years because of its tropical and humid climate—six months rainy season and six months hot and dry. Health hazards had been numerous across the years. As a boy I had had a severe case of malaria in Mississippi, and from that standpoint, Liberia, where malaria was so prevalent, was somewhat threatening. But we went with complete abandon, believing that it was the work to which God had called us. The words of John Greenleaf Whittier were never more real to us:

> I know not where His islands lift
> Their fronded palms in air;
> I only know I cannot drift
> Beyond His love and care.

We were further prepared for the venture by the Honorable Momolu Dukuly, then secretary of state of the Republic of Liberia. He was a delegate to the General Conference, and was at the Jurisdictional Conference when I was elected. He extended to us a warm welcome from President William V. S. Tubman, who was a lay preacher in the Methodist Church, and advised us on plans for travel. Due to the monsoon season from May to the middle of October, he suggested that we plan to arrive the latter part of October to begin our work there.

The trip from New York to Liberia was around thirty hours, making stops at Santa Maria, Lisbon, Dakar, and then to Robertsfield, Liberia. By comparison, it was a short trip, for it took my predecessor two weeks to make the trip in 1944. That was during World War II, and it was not safe then to travel the route which we took. The same trip today can be made nonstop in nine hours.

We were met at Robertsfield by a most cordial committee from the Liberian Church, including the secretary of state, the postmaster general, the director of public health, the mayor of Monrovia, and a number of missionaries.

The secretary of state quickly cleared us through immigration and we were on our way to Monrovia, a fifty-mile trip over a dirt road that was made soggy by the torrential rains. Although the president was on a state visit in Europe when we arrived, he had arranged for his limousine and his aide-de-camp to meet us at the airport. The driver was highly skilled in driving over those roads, so in a little more than an hour we arrived in Monrovia.

We spent the first month in an apartment in the Stokes Building, earlier used as a theological school, but at that time it was used for housing missionary families. The first few days were spent in reflection. The protocol was that we be received by the president before moving out into other parts of the country for engagements. President and Mrs. Tubman received us the day they returned and gave us a most hearty welcome. The next morning he received me in his office where we discussed the work of the church. I was greatly heartened to find him to be such a humble person, with an open mind, a deep concern for his church, profound religious convictions, and a man who held ecclesiastical leadership in high regard.

As we talked about the work of the church, I asked him for his suggestions. He replied by saying that he recognized me as the leader of the church—the ambassador of God—and he stood ready to support me in any way he could. This was a pledge he never broke in the eight years we were there.

While I had met the president when he was a state visitor in the United States in 1954, this was my first chance to really know him. He was generally maligned by the United States press, although he was America's most loyal and trusted

African friend. This, I have never understood. Mr. Tubman was a man of rare wisdom, compassionate spirit, greatly concerned about the welfare of his people, progressive in his ideas, unusually versatile, and his global understanding was refreshing.

Religion, he often said, should be the foundation of national life. He kept the doors of Liberia open to the religious organizations, and encouraged them in their work.

Although there was no episcopal residence in Liberia, President Tubman found a comfortable home for us. The Liberian people, following the lead of the president, received us with open arms. It did not take us long to realize that while there are different cultural patterns and different stages of development, people universally are essentially the same; that our ministry was not to Liberians, but to people who lived in Liberia. God has made us all one humanity. It was in that spirit that we approached our work.

In the structure of the church, Liberia occupied a rather nebulous position, being neither a Central Conference (with the authority to elect a bishop) nor a part of any other regional group. Consequently, it had no vote in any body which elected its bishops, nor any real determination of who its bishop would be. The other Methodist work in Africa (under United States supervision), the Congo (Zaire), Rhodesia, Angola, and Mozambique, was a part of the Africa Central Conference. One reason for not including Liberia was that the distance of travel would have made it impractical. Then too, Liberia was an independent republic and the others were colonies under European domination. There is a question as to whether the overlords would have received such a plan with any great enthusiasm. It was good strategy to discredit Liberia in an effort to discourage the independent movement.

Central conferences, when authorized by the General Conference, can elect their own bishop or bishops. Liberia was listed in the *Discipline* merely as "other work overseas," and the Central Jurisdiction was allotted an additional bishop to supervise the work there. In 1952, at the General Conference, Liberia applied for membership in the Central Jurisdiction with the idea that it would have some voice and vote in electing a bishop for the country. The Judicial Council declared it unconstitutional since the Central Jurisdiction was a constitutional entity in which Liberia was not included. Such an action would have required a constitutional amendment. Since efforts were being made to abolish the Central Jurisdiction, it did not seem wise to make Liberia a part of it.

There had been a lapse of two years in resident administration between the time my predecessor moved his residence to New Orleans and I moved to Liberia, and the missionaries and Liberians had become apprehensive about the future of the work. Some of them wanted precipitous action to get things going. There were others who felt they knew what should be done; they only needed a strong leader who could get it done. But there were also some who were willing to just wait and see.

I knew the danger of hasty decisions which I might later regret, so I chose to move slowly, to keep the organization essentially as I found it, and to study the situation as a whole. This was primarily my task for the first six months. Then I called together a representative group of pastors, laity, and missionaries to present the results of the study and involve them in decisions on what would be the primary emphases for the church.

President Tubman invited me to hold the meeting at the Executive Mansion so he could be there and give his support. It was a good meeting, although a rather sobering one as we considered the problems confronting us. National church ministerial leadership was by far the most serious problem. There was only one Liberian member of the Annual Conference who was a college graduate, and he was eighty years old. The Annual Conference had no funds. The rank-and-file members had little or no money, and they had not been accustomed to sharing with the church the little they had. Major programs and projects were carried on by the missionaries, with funds allocated by the Board of Missions. Liberia had been a neglected country for several years, and funds from the board were grossly inadequate.

What made this meeting so important was that the Liberians were being involved; it was not to be a program of the missionary movement. It would be the church in Liberia—missionaries and Liberians—working as a community. Prior to this meeting the program under the board was ultimately determined by the board with little, if any, reference to the Liberians themselves.

The Liberians projected some dreams of their own, and made plans to achieve them. This was an effort in which President Tubman gave noteworthy leadership. It was my conviction that Liberia's efforts to meet some of her own needs would inspire the church in the USA to contribute more freely to the work. Unfortunately, it did not happen that way. But the Liberians kept faith with their dreams, and from 1956 to 1964, raised around $750,000.

Out of these funds, 32 village schools were built, an elementary school in Monrovia was erected (the best in the nation), a science building, dormitories for boys were built at the College of West Africa, and funds were contributed to other causes. About a third of these funds were still in investments for the support of further work in the conference when I left in 1964.

The United Methodist Church had three mission stations in Liberia—Ganta, Gbarnga, and Monrovia, and about 25 missionaries. Ganta, which was 187 miles from Monrovia had, at that time, the best hospital in the country, except that of the Firestone Rubber Company. It had an elementary school, a church, and the largest leprosarium in West Africa. The work was organized in 1926 by Dr. and Mrs. George W. Harley. He was one of the most distinguished medical doctors the Board of Missions ever deployed. He was a graduate of Trinity College (now Duke University), Yale Medical School, and later earned a Ph.D. from Hartford in the field of anthropology. Mrs. Harley was a Smith College graduate. They made the trip from Monrovia to Ganta by hammocks (carried by porters). It took them three weeks to make the journey. There was no road to Ganta. Little is known of the Harleys around the world, but in my humble judgment, he did far more to lift the level of the Liberian people in their general living conditions than Albert Schweitzer did in Lambarene. Harley left the Africans an improved community, and was loved and respected throughout the country.

The station at Gbarnga, 135 miles from Monrovia, was begun in 1945 by the Liberian Annual Conference, under the administration of Bishop Willis J. King. The pioneers in the development of this mission station were a missionary black couple from Texas, Ulysses and Vivienne Gray. While they were able to get to the location by car, there was not even a house for them to live in when they arrived. Because the project was not one that the Board of Missions initiated, it took little interest in its development. The conference had raised ten thousand dollars in an effort to launch the mission, but had little or no money to carry it further. In later years, however, the board did include it in its budget for Liberia, but it was never adequately funded. It was during the latter years of my administration that the Women's Division of Christian Service gave funds for the building of a girls' dormitory, but accepted no further responsibility for the work there.

The Gbarnga mission was not the most pretentious station—always struggling to exist—but its contribution to the country was outstanding. The station had an elementary school, a church, and later a Bible training school for pastors with limited educational background. Both of the Grays were graduates of Wiley College, Austin, Texas, and Gammon Theological Seminary. It was my privilege to have taught them at Gammon, to have solemnized their marriage, and to have encouraged them to take the venture to Liberia, although I did not have the slightest idea that ten years later I would be their bishop there.

The Grays did many things at Gbarnga, but their greatest talent was producing leadership for the country. Among the persons who were sponsored by them were Melvina Nagbe, widow of Bishop Stephen Nagbe; Bishop and Mrs. Bennie Warner (Bishop Warner also became vice president of Liberia. Both offices ended with the coup dètat of 1980.); Arthur Henry, who became director of elementary schools of the Methodist Church in Liberia; and Arthur Flumo, who succeeded Bishop Warner as bishop. These are merely examples of the numerous young people they inspired and trained. The church there was one of the most active in the country.

The College of West Africa, Monrovia, is the church's oldest missionary enterprise in Liberia. The original building in which the school was housed was purchased by Melville B. Cox in 1833, the first foreign missionary of the Methodist Episcopal Church. While the school was chartered as a college, it has always been a high school, and without question, the best high school in Liberia. Many of the distinguished leaders of Liberia are graduates of it. Many of the graduates have gone to England and the United States and have been admitted to colleges and universities without conditions.

In earlier years mission stations were dotted in many sections of the country; in recent years the work of the Board of Missions has been concentrated in the three stations mentioned above. It is not my purpose to give the history of the church in Liberia. I merely give this sketch in order to interpret the nature of the work as I shared it, the problems we faced, the potentials we saw, and the efforts that were made to give new hope to the church as it grew to maturity.

The Field Committee—later the Committee on Coordination—composed of representatives of missionaries and Liberians, was an effort at consultation. In practice it proved not to be a serious involvement, since the Liberian members were told little or nothing about the total operation of programs and the finances of the various institutions.

I felt the need of the Liberians to have an understanding of the total operation of the missionary enterprise. In the first place it is their country. And further, the better they understood how the funds were being spent, and the amount of funds being received for work in Liberia, the greater would be the chances of building up a relationship of trust between the missionaries and the Liberians. Some of the older missionaries held the opinion that it would not be good for the Liberians to know, for example, the salaries and emoluments of the missionaries, since they differed widely from the Nationals who were employed in the program. But the reaction was just the opposite. When they found out what the missionaries were receiving for salaries, some thought they (the missionaries) were underpaid.

There had been the feeling originally that more money was being sent to the country from the board and that the missionaries were the chief benefactors. When they discovered this was not true, the problem was put to rest and greater mutual trust developed.

Of course, there were still many problems, among which was the employment of young Liberians on a professional basis. The salaries of missionaries were fixed and arranged by the board, but support for Nationals had to be squeezed out of the work budget. In previous years, houses built for missionaries were not available for Liberians.

It is remarkable to note the extraordinary work that was done through the missionary program in Liberia despite the serious handicaps. Perhaps it would be appropriate here to mention a few things about the work our missionaries have done around the world as I have observed and participated in it.

There are many people who have sought to classify the missionary movement merely as an agent of imperialism, robbing the natives of their rich heritage, and westernizing them with a brand of Christianity that helped to keep them obedient servants to their colonial masters. That there were certain elements of truth in some of this is undeniable. But it is a grave disservice to many dedicated persons who in many unselfish ways worked arduously for a better life for underprivileged peoples around the world.

One must never forget that it was the missionary schools that gave the early leaders of independent countries in Africa the major education they experienced. What a difference it would have made in the life of these young nations had these schools never existed! They were also basic to the young Africans who went abroad for higher education, many of whom are now or have been in the echelons of leadership in their respective countries.

The clinics and hospitals in most of these countries furnished the best, and in some instances the only, health care available.

The accusation has been frequently made that the missionaries took away from the natives their culture, and tried to brainwash them with western ideas and ways of life. There is probably an element of truth in this also, for the missionaries carried to these countries what they had learned at home, and what they had to teach was what they knew. Many of them sought, however, to learn the people, their mores, languages, and to interpret their faith against the background and understanding they found among the people. The only way for any people to remain culturally static is to live in isolation. With the infusion of other cultures, it is possible for a group to absorb some of the worst qualities and give up some of its best; but again, what they gain may at times be better than what they gave up.

Whatever may be the upheavals in some of these countries today—the outcome of which we cannot predict—we should never forget the invaluable service of some of the missionaries.

It was through the kindness of President Tubman that we had opportunities to gain insights into many parts of the world while we were in Liberia. Each time a head of state was elected in a newly independent country, President Tubman would invite the leader to Liberia for a state dinner and reception. Belle and I always received an invitation to these affairs, and we would usually sit at the president's table opposite the guests of honor. They would invite us to visit their countries, and arrange for us to meet many of their leaders of church and state. These contacts were invaluable to us in getting a broader knowledge of the continent, its history, its problems, its promises, and identifying in some measure with the agonies and hopes of the people.

We had also the opportunity of meeting, through the diplomatic corps in Monrovia, leaders from many countries around the world, who would put us in contact with leaders of their respective countries when we traveled.

Bishop Newell Booth and Bishop Ralph Dodge, who had served for many years in Central Africa, did much to help us understand the work in their respective areas, and to meet the leaders of the church.

We do not claim that these contacts made us experts on Africa, the Middle East, and other parts of the world we visited. We knew we were merely getting an introduction to the vast and complicated problems and relationships inherent in the changing political, economic, and social climate that was beginning to form. But we count ourselves fortunate to have had the experience of witnessing nations emerging into statehood, and to have shared, to some extent, their hopes and dreams. We have followed the movements of these nations at a distance, across the years.

XVI

Life in New Jersey

Mention has been made of our return to the states, and my assignment to the New Jersey area. This was another step toward the wholeness of the church, and there were many people who wanted to see the effort succeed. It was not only a new experiment assigning a black bishop to a predominantly white area, but it was also the forming of a new area out of two annual conferences, each of which had been a part of another area. The Newark Conference (now northern New Jersey) had been a part of the New York area, and the New Jersey Conference (now southern New Jersey) was a part of the Philadelphia area. The people of each conference were oriented toward the area with which the conference had been connected. Now they would have to work together. It should be noted, however, that for the first twenty years of their existence the two conferences had formed one conference (1837-1857). They then became two separate annual conferences and have remained so until this day. While the conferences were a part of the same state, they had no recent history of working together.

On the recommendation of the Episcopacy Committee of the Jurisdictional Conference of 1964, the city of Princeton was fixed as the residence or headquarters of the new area.

Princeton was probably chosen because of its rather central location in the state (located about 15 miles from Trenton, the capital). But it is more likely that Princeton was chosen because it was considered a center of culture, and would adjust more quickly to having a black bishop reside there without being discriminated against. The choice proved to be a happy one. It must be remembered, however, that this was in 1964, and Princeton was hardly further along than the initial stage of integration.

Housing was a problem, despite state real estate laws against biases. The agent who was helping us locate a house knew that it was unpopular to show houses to blacks in certain areas of the city so he sought to avoid doing it. When we insisted on seeing houses in those neighborhoods, he became busy that afternoon and had another agent take us around. She showed several houses to us that afternoon, avoiding the communities that were subtly closed to blacks. When the agent returned the next day we pressed him on the matter. He denied that there was any complicity, but finally told us that the owner of the house, which was finally bought for us, had left word not to sell it to blacks.

It would have been easy to have made an issue over the occurrence, for there were individuals and organizations just waiting for a chance to attack. I was approached several times but did not reveal that I was having a problem. It was my studied judgment that I could not be an effective leader of the area, and at the same time become the area's number one problem. We gave up buying our own home at that time, and asked the area to purchase an episcopal residence. Belle and I kept the housing problem to ourselves until ten years later when I felt the conferences were entitled to know the facts. The area committee bought the house the man did not want blacks to own.

Let me hasten to say that the neighbors were most cordial to us, and some of them are among our warmest friends. As my retirement approached, leaders of the conferences, having known our desire from the beginning to have our own home, recommended the sale of the house to us, and the conferences agreed. As I look back, I am thoroughly convinced that had the information concerning our difficulty leaked in 1964, it would have taken the spotlight, and the unity of the area may have been greatly delayed, or not achieved.

Following the session of the Jurisdictional Conference at Syracuse, the delegates of the two conferences met with Belle and me to welcome us to the area, and to inquire what help they could give us in getting adjusted. There were two immediate problems—a place to live and an office in which to work. Added to the complication was the fact that I had been assigned by the Council of Bishops to be the representative of the Council to the Latin America Central Conference, which was held a week later in Montevideo, Uraguay. I had little or no chance to make any plans before leaving. Tracey Jones, executive secretary of the World Division of the General Board of Missions, gave me office space in the board's quarters, 475 Riverside, New York City, until other arrangements could be made.

This was a tremendous advantage to me, for among other things it afforded me a temporary address where I could be reached by telephone and receive mail and persons. The district superintendents appointed a committee, at my request, to find possible places for a house and office and were to report to me on my return. It happened that the professor of Buddhology of Princeton University was taking a sabbatical leave at that time, and was subletting his home for a year. The committee had to act before I returned. It was a very nice home and was to be rented furnished. The problem was that the rent was six hundred dollars above my rental allowance. The committee, on behalf of the area, accepted the six hundred dollars as an area responsibility, and rented the house for that year. When the man and his wife showed us the house, there were a number of things they said would be accessible. When we arrived, however, they had been locked up, and the "completely furnished" meant the bare necessities. But we had our own personal effects, so it made little or no difference. It was really a favor because we did not have to worry about their belongings.

Charles Marker, pastor of Princeton Methodist Church,

made temporary office space available at the church, and the New Jersey area began to take shape. The Palmer Square Building in the center of the borough, across the street from Princeton University, was being built, and office space was being rented. When we arrived we were among the first to apply for space and were given an excellent view on the third floor facing Nassau Street and the university. It was the day after Labor Day that we moved into the new building. We were the second tenants to occupy it. The Princeton Bank and Trust Company had moved in the day before. While we did not plan it that way, we were happy to have seen the money move in ahead of us, although the only advantage we derived was convenience. This was the area headquarters for seven years. When rates climbed beyond what we conceived to be realistically appropriate to pay, we moved to the Opinion Research Building, where the rent was cheaper and the facilities equally as good.

It was Charles Marker, also, who assisted me in securing the services of Mrs. Doris Parker as secretary. How fortunate I was to have a person with such remarkable efficiency and dedication as I began the work, and to have her remain during my twelve years of administration of the New Jersey area.

One of the factors which contributed to the success of the venture was the line of able episcopal leaders who preceded me. Among the bishops of the Newark Conference were Francis J. McConnell, G. Bromley Oxnam, Frederick B. Newell, and Lloyd C. Wicke. And for twenty years, Fred P. Corson had been the guiding hand of the New Jersey Conference. Each leader had his own style, but together they left a heritage of strength and direction upon which the new area could be built. My immediate predecessors (always) extended to me a hand of friendship, and were available for counsel at points where they could be helpful. Just to have them around was a source of strength.

I can never forget the magnitude of the support of the district superintendents in helping to give shape to the area.

Although the conferences had little history of working together, the district superintendents immediately joined hands across conference lines to work toward the highest interest of the area as a whole. Under their leadership, the umbilical cords of the former areas were cut, and allegiances were transferred to the new area. An area study commission was set up to discover ways the two conferences might best work together and a number of plans were devised and implemented.

The question arose from time to time: Since New Jersey is an area, why not become one conference? The General Conference of 1836 took the following act in separating what was then the New Jersey district of the Philadelphia conference: "New Jersey Conference shall include the whole state of New Jersey, Staten Island, and so much of the states of New York, and Pennsylvania as is now included in the Asbury District." (Journal of General Conference, 1836, p. 472.) Over a period of twenty years, however, the membership practically doubled, and the conference considered dividing into two annual conferences. This was granted by the 1856 General Conference, and the Newark and New Jersey annual conferences came into being (1856, p. 107).

In 1868 overtures were made by the Newark Annual Conference to the New Jersey Annual Conference for reunion of the two conferences. Nothing resulted. In 1932, a joint committee was created to study the same matter, but in 1935, the committee was discontinued (*The Methodist Trail* in New Jersey, Frank B. Stanger, Editor, p. 10). At the time of this writing, the matter of merger is again under review by the Jurisdictional Boundaries Committee. Sound arguments can be given on each side of the issue. My own convictions are that there should not be a forced marriage by outside powers, but the conferences should be allowed to work it out for themselves. There could be a time when outside encouragement might be in order, but that time is not now.

The sixties were foreboding and difficult times. The Black Revolution was in full force. It was an era of hostilities and distrust—one in which patience was considered a vice rather than a virtue. Tempers flared and cities burned. The restlessness of the church is a chapter all in itself. It was a reflection of the social revolution. Life as usual could no longer be possible. Justice had been postponed too long and blacks were no longer willing to wait for the orderly processes of law to give relief. The laws themselves were under attack, for many of them reflected and supported the inequities against which minorities protested.

The blacks were not alone in this mood. Many whites joined in movements and demonstrations in efforts to improve the quality of life for all. There was hope on the part of some that the nonviolent approach advocated by Martin Luther King, Jr. and his followers would produce the needed social awareness to lead to reforms. Others resisted any change. But this nation was not to enjoy the luxury of orderly transition. Violence was experienced in almost every city with painful consequences.

In New Jersey, for example, Newark, Patterson, Plainfield, and Camden, among others, were seriously burned and crime was rampant. It had many ramifications, perhaps foremost among them was the attempt of the oppressed and neglected people to call attention to their plight, and express their resentment of the way they were forced to live. I remember hearing a young man gloat over the way the blacks were planning to burn the city in which he lived and worked. I asked, "What will you be doing while all this is taking place?" He replied, "I will be watching it from my window." The tragic fact is that this was an oversimplification, for not even the church was able to hide behind its stained glass windows, view the disaster, and escape the consequences. Militancy is difficult to deal with whether the cause is right or wrong.

It was in this state of condition that I was called on to live and work—to organize a new area and give it direction. I cannot forget the first press conference I had in Princeton. One of the questions a young reporter asked me was, "What are your plans to solve the race problem in New Jersey?" I tried to explain the nature of my assignment as a bishop of the church, that we did not work unilaterally, and that the church as a whole set our direction. My church had embarked on a plan and program to wipe out structural segregation in the chuch and move toward inclusiveness in its life and work. My assignment to the New Jersey area was an expression of this purpose, and my duties included taking leadership in fulfilling it.

How does one interpret in a world in revolution that his task is neither secular nor partisan, and that while his administration must take into account all issues, his true ministry should not be issue centered. It is to proclaim the wholeness of the gospel to the wholeness of the people in relationship to the wholeness of the world. It isn't easy. It sounds sometimes like an evasion of the pressing problems of the moment, or unwillingness to touch base when confronted with fundamental needs—sidestepping the significant, playing "the fiddle while Rome burns."

Then too, when crises arise some people see only one way of addressing them. When one does not ally himself with that way, he is sometimes considered indifferent, a coward, or a traitor.

A dinner reception was given for Belle and me at Drew University when we first came to the area. It was during the time when the barber shops in Madison were being picketed by some of the Drew students because of their refusal to cut the hair of black Drew students. The president of the university had joined the students in the protest and had marched with them—a noble gesture, I felt. A press conference was set up for me just before the meal. I welcomed the conference, for I was just getting started and felt this would give me a chance to interpret the work of the church and make our efforts more visible in the wider community. The main question the press asked was, "Do you support the boycott of the barber shops in Madison by the Drew students and the administration?" The deeper question of the black boys being discriminated against was not raised by them. What the press really wanted, I have always felt, was to use me in kindling the flames of hostility between the university and the community. Well, I did not afford them that luxury. I merely told them I am unalterably opposed to discrimination against anybody on the basis of race, class, religion, or any artificial consideration. But I had not been around long enough to make any assessment as to whether the boycott was the best method to open up the shops. The press did not attend the dinner and hear my statement there, so my coverage in the morning papers consisted of a poorly taken picture and few lines indicating that I was around. The point, however, is that it is so easy to assume that when one is not supportive of a method, he is not supportive of a goal, or vice versa.

There were times when I had some difficulty making my positions clear among the blacks. They had been standing in line for a century, waiting for the door of opportunity to be opened. My assignment, they reasoned, was the key if I just had the courage to use it—appoint black district superinten- dents and black pastors to affluent white churches, and to conference-wide positions. There were problems, of course. For some reason I have never understood, our denomination never drew large numbers of blacks in New Jersey, and their churches were relatively small. The larger churches were farther south in Pennsylvania, Maryland, and Washington. Consequently, they drew the stronger leaders. I faced a dearth of black leadership and I could not move as fast as would have been feasible in some other sections of the church. This was accepted at times as hesitation on my part to act decisively on the race issue and move ahead in breaking down barriers. There was pressure in the area, and among blacks within the churches to move ahead. I just refused to do it, for I felt it to be as unethical to place a person in a position where one did not have the capacity to function effectively as it is to deny that person the opportunity when the qualifi- cations are not the issue. It harms the person as well as the cause. When I found that I had qualified persons to fill these positions I placed them as persons, not as racial symbols. There was a brief period in which my position was not accepted with any degree of hospitality among blacks, and some sought to even punish me. It was short-lived, however, and when my basic operating principle was more clearly understood, I won many friends who respected me for the stand that I took.

Governor Richard Hughes of the state of New Jersey included me as a member of a study commission on civil disorder following the unrest in the cities. A member of the staff of the General Board of Church and Society, on hearing of the appointment, came from Washington to Princeton to discuss the appointment with me and to offer his services in any way I thought he could be helpful. He assumed that the government would seek to control the outcome of the report, and perhaps try to cover up important data. In the course of the conversation he said to me, "There are a number of people who feel that you do not have the courage to leak to the press any relevant material that the public has a right to have." I said, "Let us turn the statement around. I have too much courage to sabotage a report and make unauthorized and secret statements to the press." Then, I wanted to know on what basis did he prejudge the work of the commission or the integrity of the governor. The staff member was a good person and his intentions were good, but this indicates how the level of trust had broken down, and the extent to which respectable people will go to win a point in a crisis.

James Forman appeared in Riverside Church, New York City to present the Black Manifesto, demanding reparation for the deprivations suffered by blacks in the past. It was reported that Forman took the microphone from the pastor as he was delivering his sermon, and presented his own document to the congregation. Groups visited church headquarters and similar places making their demands.

Word came to me that Forman had plans to visit the Northern New Jersey Conference in its session at Drew

University, 1969, during Holy Communion, and take over the service from me inasmuch as I was considered a black out of step with the movement. We made adequate preparation for his arrival, and sent him advance notice of what we would do if he came; he changed his mind. Nevertheless, I felt it was my duty to say to the conference that there had been considerable searching of heart by the major Protestant denominations over the Black Manifesto with which Forman had confronted national boards and organizations, and had sought to force acquiescence by the threat of reprisals. Although no board had responded directly to his demands, I was puzzled by the recognition he was given, for it seemed to indicate what could happen to the church when caught up in a mingled feeling of fear and guilt.

I indicated that I would be among the first to complain that the blacks in America have been grossly mistreated, and the correction of these evils should be on the agenda of church and state as long as the evils exist. It is mandatory that this country turn attention to these problems in a serious way. But James Forman did not have the plan nor the goal toward which the church should be working. And the church should have the courage to stand up and say so. It is my conviction that many conference members took courage and began to put the whole matter in proper perspective, and gain a new sense of responsibility. The motivation had to be faith in Christ and not fear of reprisals if any vital and creative response was to be made. Some of these self-appointed individuals and groups were exploiting a bad situation for their own personal gains, and some people were falling into the trap.

That there were reasons to protest there is no doubt, and anger was understandable. It is also true that the church had allowed itself to fall into a predicament where it seemed able only to react to protests, instead of being in the vanguard of social change and a better way of life for all people. It is so easy for the church to abandon its role as the conscience of the state and become its colleague. And "Where there is no prophecy, the people get out of hand. . . ." (Proverbs 29:18).

Acquiescence to a short-term escape is never an ultimate solution to a significant problem. A quick fix disintegrates quickly, and the condition usually worsens. This is true because little or nothing is being done to eliminate the basic cause.

There are those who go overboard in an effort to keep a false peace. Time after time, I have heard whites comment after voting for something just because blacks proposed it, "Well, I didn't really go along, but to oppose it is like opposing motherhood." We must learn to be completely open to one another on matters that may even extract some pain. When we play games, each side usually knows it, and the element of trust continually declines. With this approach, the gap between races widens and the critical problems deepen. Black and white must learn to plan and work together in the common interest of God's community. Without this, we can never reach the level of being his church.

During our twelve years of active duty in the New Jersey area, we were greatly encouraged by the increasing number of people who sought, with integrity, ways of reaching out to one another in fellowship and understanding—to be the body of Christ.

XVII

Boards and Agencies

When I returned from Liberia in 1964, one of my greatest desires was to serve on the General Board of Missions, especially the world division. I had worked closely with the board and had some firsthand knowledge and experience with the needs and hopes of the people. Because of my eight-year assignment outside the United States, my relationships with the bishops of the central conferences were most congenial, for we had common problems. There were times when I sought to interpret these situations in the Council of Bishops. I coveted the privilege, therefore, of being a member of the board where many of the basic decisions were made concerning the work commonly called "overseas."

Among the fifteen bishops from the United States named by the Council of Bishops to the board, four had been directly involved with the work of the board. Charles F. Golden and W. Vernon Middleton had been with the national division staff before their election to the Episcopacy; Newell S. Booth had served as a missionary in Central Africa, and for twenty years as bishop there; and I had been in West Africa. The board had the authority to assign the board members to the respective divisions, departments, and committees where it thought they could best serve. While I have never understood the rationale, Newell Booth and I were put in the national division, and Charles Golden and Vernon Middleton were assigned to the world division. This was done without any consultation with any one of us as far as I know.

I was assigned to the Committee on Architecture, which really put me on freeze. This was an area in which I did not have any contribution to make; I cannot read a blueprint and I cannot drive a nail straight. I just decided I would not embarrass the committee by attending its meetings, and at the end of the quadrennium, I asked to be changed to another board.

There were times when I wondered if there were not a board point of view, and any different position was unwelcome, whatever might have been its logic. When I was in Liberia, I frequently differed with the board's policies and decisions (as I still do), and felt there were no reasons to be timid in making my views known. It may have been that I was naïve about the fundamental principal of democracy in which the free expression of conscience is encouraged.

Of course, there is a certain built-in inflexibility in any bureaucracy, and though it may listen at times, it is difficult for it to hear. It is possible also for the signals to become confusing, and the agency has to move ahead on its own convictions. Despite our problems the role of missions in the United Methodist Church has been one of the most outstanding of any Protestant communion. I have followed the trails of missionaries around the world, and have been moved by their dedication and commitment. Missionaries at times have been greatly maligned. This is true partly because of the twisted concepts concerning them. Missionaries abroad are church people who have felt the call to work in distant lands and cultures, but are just as prone to human error as church people anywhere. Therefore, some fall by the wayside; some get discouraged and leave their assignment; some go with wrong attitudes and never overcome them. The efforts of some have been non-productive, and sometimes negative. But many of them have been outstanding witnesses to the Christian faith under the most taxing and difficult circumstances.

XVIII

The Church International

The organization of the Commission on the Structure of Methodism Overseas, 1948, was the beginning of a new direction for the Methodist Church. Its original purpose was "to study the work and supervision of the Methodist Church in its work outside of the United States and its territories, and its relationship to other church bodies, and prepare such recommendations as it considers necessary for presentation to the General Conference. . . ." No one at that time could foresee the course these churches would ultimately take.

On the surface it seemed that the structure of the church merely needed a certain amount of overhauling as issues arose in the field, but later events suggested that the problems were deeper. For the first sixteen years of the commission's existence the recommendations were rather routine and nominal. But in the 60s, when nationalism was at its height, and the independence movement around the world was in full surge, the churches outside the United States began to raise serious questions as to whether they could any longer leave the decisions that affected them on a national level to be made by a body which was primarily geared to serve the United States.

It was in 1964 that I became a member of the commission. Bishop Richard C. Raines, chairman, was a person who not only had a broad understanding of the problems, but also had the confidence of the church leaders outside the United States. He was willing and able to lead the commission in search of a broad understanding of the underlying issues and had an openness to the future. As chairman of the Committee on Legislation of the Commission, it was my responsibility to give leadership to framing whatever legislation was to be presented to the General Conference.

We discovered early in the process, however, that broad legislation presupposed a more careful and penetrating study than had ever been made—to examine assumptions that had just been taken for granted. We raised the issue, for example, "Is the Methodist Church a world church at work in forty countries around the world? Or is it an American church with appendages outside the United States?" In facing this question, we had to come to grips with the fact that the work outside the United States began as a missionary enterprise which developed as missionaries carried the gospel across the world. It was not started with a world comprehensive plan. Some missionaries went out with self-support, and others found support back home, but it was not a church planned movement. Schools, hospitals, and other needed service institutions were developed as a part of their work.

The Methodist Church, therefore, in time came to have units in many lands. The question arose of how to relate these institutions to the church at home. The first efforts were assumed by the bishops, who as general superintendents would send one from their group to visit a field, perhaps once a year. As the work grew and annual conferences developed, these conferences were given membership in the General Conference, with representation on the same basis as the annual conferences in the United States. The bishops held conferences and ordained the preachers. But the annual visitation of a bishop to these remote and isolated places proved unsatisfactory. The first missionaries were members of annual conferences in the United States and were appointed to these posts by the bishops. The bishops rotated in these assignments and there was no particular follow-up by a single bishop. It would be a mistake to conclude that these episcopal visitations were not significant, for the work of some of them is still clearly evident.

In order to meet the complaint of remote supervision, episcopal residences were established, and bishops were elected and assigned to these various fields. At the General Conference of 1920, fourteen men were elected, largely for service overseas.

The Methodist Episcopal Church, South resolved the problem by setting up autonomous churches. In 1930 this was done in Japan, Mexico, Korea, and Brazil, and only a supportive relationship was continued. At the time of union in 1939, the churches remaining under the aegis of the old mission field system were China, Cuba, and the Congo (now Zaire). But the Methodist Episcopal Church still continued the world church concept, and continued to make accommodations for its administration. Thus the Central Conference system emerged about the time of union in 1939. It gave opportunity for the election of bishops from their native land and also made possible the adaptation of certain legislation to local conditions. All bishops of Central Conferences, however, were not Nationals. A number of American missionaries were elected by the Central Conferences and gave yeoman leadership to the churches. But the trend was toward the election of Nationals. The church had reached maturity and it needed this chance to elect its own national leaders.

There were handicaps in this system. One was the limited recognition given to the Central Conference bishops. They were considered local bishops, not general superintendents, as were the bishops elected by jurisdictional conferences in the United States. A bishop's authority was operative only in the Central Conference that elected him, or in other central conferences if requested by them. He was a member of the Council of Bishops, but could vote only on issues pertaining to Central Conference matters. The *Discipline* of 1944 states this clearly: "The bishops of the Central Conferences shall have membership in the Council of Bishops with vote limited to matters relating to their respective conference."

"The Bishops of the Central Conferences shall preside in the sessions of their respective Central Conferences" (The Constitution, #20.2-3). They were not eligible to preside in the General Conference nor any conferences beyond their boundaries. A bishop elected by a Jurisdictional Conference could preside anywhere.

Another matter of profound significance was the question of local administration. While the bishop was theoretically in charge, the Board of Missions was in control. It was originally a supportive organization, but later became, for all practical purposes, one that determined significant decisions in the field. This was an underlying factor which prompted the Central Conference bishops to request an agency through which they could take their problems directly to the General Conference. Out of this prompting came the Commission on the Structure of Methodism Outside the United States (COSMOS). (The change precipitated from a discussion of who is overseas from whom.) A commission on Central Conferences was named by the Council of Bishops as early as 1944 (Bishop Roy H. Short, *History of the Council of Bishops,* p. 53).

There was only one board which reached beyond the American borders—the Board of Missions. That there were some justifiable reasons for this arrangement did not alter the fact that the overseas people felt they were outside the church as a whole, with little leverage in changing policies and influencing administration. Since the concentration of Methodist population was in the United States, 95% of the delegates to General Conferences were from this country.

The difficult problem to deal with was that of administration, and the *Discipline* was not always too clear on the definition of responsibility. Since much of the legislation, in the early years, was proposed by the Board of Missions, perhaps the board deemed it wise to keep the legislation flexible so it could make determinations in keeping with its goals and purposes.

COSMOS examined a number of suggestions of how the

Methodist Church might become, structurally, a world church in which every segment would have peer relationships. But the time had passed for such considerations, for eight conferences in Latin America and four in Asia had requested autonomy, which was granted at the General Conference of 1968. Whether or not this exit could have been avoided had earlier developments been along a different line is mere conjecture. Personal ambitions in some instances may have played a role, and in other instances it seemed to have been an element of "having the cake and eating it, too." One has to take into account, also, the pressures of nationalism at that time. The predominant factor appeared to be that the leaders of the conferences were tired of a second-class status in the church.

There had been improvements along the way, but they were too little as well as too late. Central Conference bishops gained full rights in the Council of Bishops, (due to rulings of the Jurisdictional Council), and in 1956 Bishop J. Waskom Pickett from India, elected in 1936, presided at the General Conference the evening that the focus was on India. He was the first Central Conference bishop to preside over a General Conference.

In 1968, when Bishop Raines retired, I was elected chairman of the commission. Robert Martin, a former missionary to Brazil, was chosen as staff secretary and gave invaluable service to the commission. It was under Bishop Raines' leadership that the General Conference gave approval to the commission, in consultation with the Council of Bishops, to hold a series of jurisdictional meetings, so that the United Methodists within the United States would have an opportunity to discuss structure issues affecting the total church. The Central Conferences had already had a chance to discuss these issues, under the leadership of COSMOS, prior to the General Conference.

The General Conference also provided funds for a World Methodist Congress, which was held in Atlantic City, New Jersey, April, 1970. The congress was composed of around three hundred delegates from the jurisdictions, Central conferences, autonomous churches, sister churches, and other invited persons. The congress lasted five days and many ideas of new relationships and structures emerged. It is not my purpose to go into details of the congress. It was held in the attitude of prayer, and many who attended felt that the Holy Spirit governed the deliberations. But proposals for federal or organic structures were not received with any real enthusiasm.

There was the general feeling, however, that the churches belonged together, if not in a formal organization, then in a fellowship of understanding and cooperation. The congress finally concluded that the World Methodist Council, radically restructured, would be the most satisfactory arrangement for that fellowship and cooperation on a world level. A joint committee representing COSMOS and the World Methodist Council was appointed to work out plans for the restructuring. The World Methodist Council, meeting in Denver, 1971, and the General Conference, 1972, both approved the plans. COSMOS decided that there was no further need for its existence; therefore it recommended to the General Conference that the commission be discontinued, and that a Central Conference affairs committee be organized to handle any matters relating to the Central Conferences that still remained in The United Methodist Church.

The primary concern that COSMOS had with the World Methodist Council was the lack of a broad representation in its work on a global basis. While the council had existed since 1881, its leadership was generally an exchange between the Anglo Saxons in America and Great Britain. The former Central Conferences, now autonomous, had sought a peer relationship which the present structure did not provide, and it was the task of the committee to devise a structure that would be mutually acceptable. Considerable discussion took place in the Executive Committee of the World Methodist Council concerning any changes to accommodate these churches, with the main resistance coming from the British, since these autonomous churches were American related, not British related. As chairman of COSMOS, I was invited to the Executive Committee meeting held in Helsinki, Finland, to interpret the work of COSMOS. The Executive Committee decided that it would be helpful for me to be a member of it so that I could be a part of all discussions. I had been a member of the council since 1956. The council normally meets every five years, and the Executive Committee, which meets annually, is empowered to carry on the work between sessions of the council.

My presence on the committee was not without concern, especially by the British. They viewed me as having the best of two worlds, for to them COSMOS was another international organization, somewhat in competition with the World Methodist Council. It did not matter how much I tried to explain that COSMOS was a commission of The United Methodist Church, limited to the work of the church, and responsible directly to the General Conference. It did not make sense to them, since we were involved in the future relationship of the affiliated autonomous churches. I have often wondered if the name COSMOS, easily mistaken for cosmos, meaning world, was not a part of the problem. The British did not have any such counterpart, and therefore, understanding for them was difficult. The atmosphere was emotionally charged, which made objective hearing not easy. The breakthrough was troublesome, but was finally achieved.

Dr. Charles Parlin was chairman of the joint committee, of which I was co-chairman, to work out proposals for a new structure. It was soon decided that in any new structure, peer relationships on all levels and for every church body should be provided for. This could best be done through the Executive Committee. The final proposal, which was adopted, was that "Each church shall be entitled to at least one member on the Executive Committee, and no two member churches shall together command a majority of the seats of the Executive Committee." This provision was included to assure that The United Methodist Church and the British Methodist Church, the two largest groups, could not numerically dominate the Executive Committee.

Instead of one president for the body, as was the historical practice, a presidium was established of "not more than eight (8) presidents, no two (2) of which shall come from the same member church, and which collectively shall constitute a presidium, which shall include one laywoman, one layman, and one youth. . . ." This was a further effort to broaden the base of representation, for as presidents, they are officers in the council (with other officers which the constitution provides for) and preside at ceremonial occasions at the meeting of the council.

Along with the presidium, the new structure provides for a chairman of the Executive Committee invested with the responsibility "for oversight of the administration of the World Methodist Council between sessions of the Executive Committee, and shall have the right from time to time to delegate authorities to a Vice Chairman of the Executive Committee."

The choice of a chairman became a problem. The nominating committee was unanimous in its nomination of myself, but it provoked considerable discussion by some members of the British delegation who still felt that I was already head of a world organization (COSMOS). A number of schemes and tactics were used to defeat my election, such as proposing structural changes that would make it illegal. For example, it was proposed and adopted that the chairman and treasurer cannot come from the same member church. A very valuable treasurer of long standing in the council was already from The United Methodist Church. He immediately resigned, thereby removing that roadblock. When the nominating committee made its report, there was an effort made from the floor to substitute the name of Bishop Yap Kim Howe of Singapore for mine, but the motion was defeated. When the vote was finally taken I was elected by an overwhelming majority.

I am happy to say that once the election was over, the British supported my administration, and the work went well. Dr. Lee F. Tuttle, who had been general secretary since 1961, continued in that position until his retirement in 1976. His grasp of the work of the council, and his broad ecumenical understanding was invaluable as the council embarked on its new structure and program.

In the World Methodist Council there are sixty-three member churches, active in ninety countries. They have almost twenty-four registered members and represent a total community of fifty-one million adherents.

In 1976, Dr. Kenneth Greet of England succeeded me, and in 1981, Bishop William R. Cannon, USA, succeeded him. The work has continued to grow in strength as a community of fellowship and cooperation on a world level.

The council played an important part in the restoration of Wesley's Chapel, London. The celebration of the century-old restored building, November, 1978, was honored by the presence of Her Majesty the queen, and the reading of one of the Scripture lessons by His Royal Highness.

Because the new organization possessed similarities to the World Council of Churches, there were some who thought that the World Methodist Council might be an effort to compete with the World Council of Churches. Their fears were soon allayed, for there has not been any effort to be a substitute for the interfaith organization or to duplicate its work. In fact, the strength of the family organization supplements the goals and purposes of the World Council of Churches, and most of the member churches are members of it also.

The degree of autonomy which the Central Conferences of The United Methodist Church have qualifies them to be members of the Council on the same basis as the autonomous Methodist and United churches.

Dr. Joe Hale was elected to succeed Dr. Tuttle at the meeting of the council, 1976. His leadership has been farsighted and brilliant, and international interest in the council continues to increase. More people around the world are involved directly in its work than ever before, and its influence is being felt increasingly.

It was in 1968 that I became involved in the work of the chaplaincy of The United Methodist Church as a member of the commission. It was under the leadership of bishops during World War II that this commission was brought into existence. The council responded to the need for chaplains in the Armed Forces. The commission was an agency directly related to the council and for which the council took great responsibility. In 1944 the *Discipline* merely carried the names of the members of the commission, and it was only in the 1948 *Discipline* that there was a definition of the commission and its responsibilities.

The duties of the commission were to "represent the Methodist Church in securing chaplains for the armed services and the Veterans Administration, in granting the required ecclesiastical endorsement, in maintaining contact with and general oversight of Methodist chaplains in reference to their ecclesiastical status while in government service, and in rendering such other services to the chaplains as may from time to time be referred to it by the Council of Bishops" (#1595, 1948). It provided also that a bishop should be the chairman. This arrangement subsisted for the first twenty-eight years of its existence, but was changed in 1972 with the new structure of the church.

The major concern of the General Conference in 1944, it appears, was the relationship of the Christian church to war. The conference passed a resolution in which it observed: "In this country we are sending over a million young people from Methodist homes to participate in the conflict. God himself has a stake in the struggle, and he will uphold them as they fight forces destructive of the moral life of man. . . ." In another resolution, it spoke in the interest of conscientious objectors. The resolution concluded: "We must assert for every person in the world, of whatever race, color, or nation, those very rights which we prize for ourselves. . . ." Strong words at a time when the American army was segregated, the nation was segregated, and five years after the Methodist Church had emerged with a plan that constitutionally segregated the blacks—a constitution which persisted for twenty years. Perhaps the church was beginning to take another look at the world scene and the barriers that tend to divide us.

The chaplaincy was another matter. It was not the creation of a force merely to build morale for fighting. It was the church selecting and supporting pastors (chaplains) to be where the millions of young people were, to sustain them. There is no doubt that the attitude of the church toward war has changed since those days, but the spiritual, social, and psychological needs of the young people who are called upon to do military services remain the same. It is so easy to get one's attitude toward war confused with the responsibility of the church to have pastors wherever the people are. My own conviction is that all wars are evil, and the nation's involvement in them at best, is the selection of a lesser evil, and not a higher good. But I could never oppose the presence of the church through its chaplains, carrying the word of God to our military forces around the world. The chaplains represent the ministry at home, and there are always those who do not measure up to the high standards set for them by the church. There is, too, a danger of a chaplain who advances in rank, taking on a military posture, and becoming more an arm of the military than a shepherd of the people. But the vast number of these chaplains with whom I was related as a member of the commission for eight years, and as its chairman for four, are among the finest ministerial leaders in the church. Whenever it has been my privilege to visit chaplains, and I have done so around the world—in retreats, in their homes, and in private consultations with them—I have usually come away humbled by their faith, courage, commitment, spirit of sacrifice, and endurance. Through them, the church is reaching out.

Whether we like it or not, the military is organized on the

basis of rank, and it is far more likely to listen to a head of the church than one who is not. As a bishop, I have been able to interpret to generals the meaning of the chaplaincy as our church sees it: that the chaplains are not military personnel under the aegis of the church that endorses them; they are ministers of the gospel, who are appointed by the church, followed up by the church, and can be withdrawn by the church. The chaplains are always pleased when a bishop of the church visits them and confers with their commanding officer.

The executive secretaries, from the commission's inception—Dr. S. Stewart Patterson, Dr. John McLaughlin, and Dr. A. Purnell Bailey—drew on the resources of the bishops in planning and executing the work of the chaplains.

The relationship of the chaplains with the council was greatly limited by the new structure of the church, which was adopted in 1972. It discontinued the Commission on Chaplains, and combined the work with the Board of Higher Education and Ministry, under the title, Division of Chaplains and Related Ministries of the Board of Higher Education and Ministry, with all ties cut with the Council of Bishops.

The dominant interest of the new board was not the chaplaincy, to say the least, and carrying on the work became increasingly difficult. For reasons I have never understood, the associate secretary, who had proven his extraordinary gifts and graces for the job, became the political target of the general secretary, which made his work extremely difficult. In spite of this he carried to the chaplains and their families a pastoral ministry for which they gave their expressions of trust and gratitude. The chaplains who knew him will always remember him and his wife with deep affection. What direction the supervision and care of the chaplains and their families will be in the future is yet to be seen.

XIX

The Episode at Drew

Drew University, Madison, New Jersey, has occupied an important place in the Methodist Church. Founded in 1866, it became the first and only theological seminary to be established by the General Conference, and the first to operate entirely on the professional graduate level. For the first one hundred years, the trustees were elected by the General Conference. It became the official depository of the Methodist Episcopal Church. It has drawn to its faculty across the years celebrated scholars, and has produced some of the church's most distinguished leaders. While still a seminary, it built up what (at that time) was considered a fair endowment.

Although Drew was chartered as a university, it operated exclusively as a theological seminary until 1928. Brothers College (now the College of Liberal Arts) was made possible by the benefaction of Leonard D. and Arthur J. Baldwin, and the school became in fact a university. Brothers College was named in honor of these two brothers who gave the funds for its establishment.

While the young college held out great potential as a feeder for the School of Theology, it was this potential which later became a source of delicate relationships and ultimate conflict. I was assigned as resident bishop of the New Jersey area at the time these crises were emerging. During the sixties, campus life was unsettled at best, and almost any difficulty could be a catalyst for disaster.

Such an incident was created by a young social science teacher whose last name was Mellon, when he announced to his class that he was a Communist. The press gave it wide publicity. Some of the trustees were confounded, and demanded quick action. An emergency meeting of the Board of Trustees was called. I received word at 11:00 in the morning that there would be a meeting that afternoon at 2:00 to deal with this matter.

Dr. Robert F. Oxnam, president of the university, knew the mood of the campus, and the readiness of students and faculty to defend academic freedom. He felt that the best approach to deal with the issue would be on academic grounds, instead of allowing political considerations to enter in. Mellon was a lecturer, and under the bylaws of the university a lecturer's services could be discontinued by the president on the recommendation of the dean involved. It did not require trustee action. Mellon did not hold a doctorate, and was employed under the condition that he receive the degree by a certain time. He had failed to meet the deadline. In addition to his teaching at Drew he had accepted a teaching assignment with the New School of Social Work in New York without clearing it with the dean. This was a breach of contract. The president recommended that Mellon be allowed to complete the semester at Drew and then be released for not having completed the academic requirements. But some of the trustees felt that Mellon should be expelled from the faculty immediately in order to clear the good name of Drew, and they insisted that the trustees take the initiative, and make it abundantly clear that the trustees would not tolerate a professed Communist on the faculty. The meeting reached an impasse. Emotions were high.

Donald Baldwin, nephew of the Baldwin brothers, and also a benefactor of the university, was chairman of the board. He was a man for whom I had enormous respect. He called on me, as head of The United Methodist Church in the New Jersey area, to comment on the matter. At this point, any comment was risky. I recalled what I said to my wife at lunch when she asked me what I wanted for dessert. I said, "Nothing, we are going to have Mellon at Drew." I began by telling them about this conversation. The laughter seemed to break through the tension.

My further comments were that, "Mellon has done the university a grave disservice, and if I were to follow my emotions I would join in putting him off the campus immediately and without ceremony. However, this is a time for poise and clear thinking which leads me to the following conclusions:

1. We are acting with greater force than is necessary. It does not require an atomic bomb to kill a fly.

2. We are giving this man more attention than he deserves. We ought not allow ourselves to become his Public Relations agents. Let us not popularize him on the campus and through the press and make him either a martyr or a national hero.

3. Since Mellon is a lecturer and not a professor, it does not require the action of the Board to dismiss him. Why risk unnecessary action that could lead to further disruption?

4. The president of the university has proposed a plan for handling the matter which appears to be wise, why not follow it? Should the board veto his recommendation, it would constitute a vote of no confidence in the president's administration, undermining his leadership at a time when it should be strengthened."

The president of the board appointed me as chairman of a committee of five. He excused us to meet and formulate a recommendation for the board to consider. The recommendation of the committee was to follow the plan of the president. The board accepted it, and we went on to other business.

Peace and quiet were not of long duration. The next time it was a conflict between the president of the university and the dean of the School of Theology. But the causes were probably much deeper. When the college was young and the students few, it was considered a complement to the School of Theology—a source of student recruitment. In time, however, the college enrollment became much larger than that of the School of Theology, and became a competitor for recognition and funds.

In 1963, Charles Ranson was invited to Drew as dean of the School of Theology. He had an impressive manner, was self-assured, and persuasive. He quickly won the confidence and loyalty of his faculty as he sought to represent them in their claim for greater consideration on the campus, especially for needed funds.

One matter of contention was the unified budget that the university had adopted. The faculty felt that it was being deprived of funds it would receive if the money were kept separate. There was the deep suspicion that the college was profiting from funds that rightly belonged to the theological school—interest from endowments and current contributions from annual conferences and other sources. A careful auditing of the funds revealed that the School of Theology, in fact, was getting considerably more for operation out of the unified budget than the total amount of funds specifically earmarked for the divinity school. Despite the audit, the dean continued to hold the position that funds for theological study were being misappropriated, and he threatened to go to the press. While some of us talked him out of that approach, word began to spread that the School of Theology had become the step-child at Drew, and funds were being misused.

At a special meeting the Executive Committee invited the dean, and any of his faculty he chose, to discuss the finances. They came, but the dean said at that time they were not doubting the fairness of the handling of financial matters, but proposed the separation of the School of Theology as a corporate entity from the university. The proposal was not favorably considered.

The tactics of the dean changed. He began to threaten to resign each time he approached the president on finances or any other issues on which the president did not agree. It finally became almost daily routine. The Executive Committee told the president to accept his resignation the next time he offered it, which the president did. The dean had no intention of resigning. He insisted that the president write him a letter, requesting his resignation. The president wrote the letter, and the explosion came. The faculty wrote a letter threatening to resign as a body if the dean were dismissed. The dean and his faculty received the support of the alumni and the national theological community.

A meeting of the board of trustees was called to consider the matter. I shall never forget that meeting. The trustees were divided. It was a moment of great crisis. Such distinguished board members as Bishop Herbert Welch, then over a hundred years old; Bishop Fred B. Newell; and Bishop Lloyd C. Wicke opposed the resolution presented by Dr. Charles C. Parlin to dismiss the dean. They expressed the conviction that a better way to handle the crisis should be sought. But Bishop Fred P. Corson and I supported the resolution, and it was supported by a vast majority of the trustees.

Harold Bosley, then pastor of Christ United Methodist Church, New York City, a member of the board who vigorously opposed the resolution, wrote me a note following the meeting in which he said he thought I would live to regret the speech I made supporting the dismissal of the dean. My response was, "Let us wait and see." I knew that it was a risk politically, but to me a basic administrative principle was involved. It is interesting to note that my same friend, Harold, three years later wrote me another note stating that he had misjudged the situation and that history was proving that I was right. Again, my reply was: "Let us wait and see."

But it was a rocky road, and much transpired between those two notes. There were the student uprisings and wholesale faculty resignations, which brought me from Princeton and other trustees to Drew night after night through rain and snow. Since the General Conference elected the trustees, and my name was up for reelection for another term, an alumnus challenged the list of nominees on the

General Conference floor and moved substitutions. The matter was referred to a committee for resolution. No significant change took place as far as the trustee membership was concerned. The gesture did inform the board of its own predicament of having an arrangement by which it could be voted out of existence by any session of a General Conference without even having a chance to present the facts.

The disruption at Drew had some positive effects, however. The board saw the necessity of taking a new look at itself and the governing process. This required a charter revision of the school, which was the first since its founding in 1866. It also required action by the state legislature, and involved some risks in tax-exempt status, which was granted in perpetuity under the old Drew charter. Fortunately, the tax-exempt status was not affected. The following revisions were made in the new charter: (1) the election of the trustees was placed solely in the hands of the trustees, with no reference to the General Conference, (2) The United Methodist Church relationship with the university was secured by including in the charter the three bishops of the contiguous areas, namely, New Jersey, New York, and Philadelphia as members of the Board of Trustees, (3) The ecumenical basis of board membership was expanded, thus making it possible to draw on a wider range of talent and experience, (4) The board invited faculty and student committees to participate in rewriting the charter and bylaws. It was here that, although with initial difficulty, the channels of communication began to open up. Strangely enough, the students were in the vanguard at this point. The faculty came along slowly. When the documents were completed, however, they had the approval of all, after a number of compromises.

It was not easy to secure a successor to Dean Ranson; the theological community across the nation was informally organized against the trustees. But in spite of pressure and discouragement, James M. Ault (now Bishop Ault) accepted the challenge, and it was not long before the school was moving off in a new and positive direction. What could have happened to the School of Theology had Ault, or someone of his caliber, not been secured is an unpleasant thought. Perhaps the greatest testimony to his leadership is that after three years, he was elected to the episcopacy.

The struggle did not end here. When the Evangelical United Brethren and the Methodist Church merged in 1968, the combined number of seminaries was more than the church needed to train its ministry. The General Conference appointed a commission to study the matter and bring a report to the conference of 1972. The commission drew certain arbitrary lines and made certain projections. It grouped, for example, Duke, Wesley, Drew, and Boston together, and suggested that there was need for not more than three theological schools in this region. Drew, the weakest from the standpoint of student enrollment, was the immediate target. It is a long story. But when the report was finally made, Drew had survived. At the time of this writing it is one of the most progressive schools of theology in the nation.

Despite the arduous struggle and misunderstandings, I was greatly humbled that in 1972, with the blessings of the faculty and the unanimous endorsement of the board of trustees, this university, which had previously conferred only a few honorary degrees, conferred upon me the degree of Doctor of Humane Letters.

XX

The Life of My Years

In writing this book I have tried to avoid the temptation of keeping my focus completely on the past, and of judging human possibilities largely on the basis of what has already transpired, whether good or bad. It is so easy to idolize the past, concluding that "there were giants in those days," and that the glory of living was then, not now. The past is mixed, as life always is, and we have to view it in the light of the whole historic movement. We cannot erase it, whatever may be our desire. It is fixed as a point of departure for the life that is still before us. One of Shakespeare's characters says, "What is past is prologue."

We are heirs to many values that have come down to us across the centuries, many of which are beyond our merits. They are a sacred trust and we are under obligation to preserve, refine, and revitalize them for the generations yet unborn. But to conserve the values does not necessarily mean that we use the same forms and methods our forebears used, "New occasions teach new duties," but the new duties are not without guidelines and lights which reflect on the road upon which we are called to travel.

There is also the tendency of some to blame the problems and difficulties we encounter on the generations who lived before us. True enough, my generation inherited a church that had been fragmented by strife and splintered by various positions and points of view. The issues of race and human slavery were root causes of much of it. Emanating from them were the black churches of Methodist origin—the African Methodist Episcopal Church (beginning as early as 1796). Whatever way one wished to interpret it, it was the issue of race that caused the spin-off. There were blacks who always remained with the mother church (Methodist Episcopal Church), who legally were a part of the full church, but in practice a segregated part, in ways that I have depicted earlier.

The issue of church oversight and administration was one which finally led to the withdrawal of a group in 1828 to form the Methodist Protestant Church. In 1844, a group withdrew from the Methodist Episcopal Church on the question of slavery and organized the Methodist Episcopal Church, South. In the merger of the three churches in 1939, segregation became a legal part of the structure, since the Central Jurisdiction (the only jurisdiction defined by race), was fixed in the Constitution of the church in a way that took twenty-seven years to remove it completely. Women were not granted full clergy rights for the first 172 years of the church's existence. These references reflect the long struggle of the church for wholeness and some of the difficulties in achieving it. The struggle still persists in many ways.

But this is also the church of the Wesleyan spirit, of Francis Asbury, the Circuit Riders, and a host of pioneers who preached scriptural holiness across the continent, and later, across the world, and across the years, bringing men and women to a new awareness of what it means to live a good life. It is the church of thousands of persons who have sought to "do good, love mercy, and walk humbly with God." We need to know the path the church has trod in order to guide and guard our steps, conserving her values, and avoiding her mistakes, lest we lose the values and repeat the errors.

The church, as I have observed it over the last half century, has come a long way at many points. I recall, for instance, the struggle the North and South had in the early days after the merger. There was yet to be developed an atmosphere of trust. Things that are now taken for granted were carefully arranged so that one side could not take advantage of the other. There were two publishing agents for the publishing interest of the church for several years—one from the South and one from the North. Care was taken also by other boards and agencies to see that representation was well-balanced. The dichotomy between North and South is no longer significantly evident.

In the selection of leadership on the general church level, being black is no longer a handicap. It is interesting to observe that three blacks were the first ones to be elected bishops in 1980 in each of the three jurisdictions that elected them.

Women are being recognized as never before in the echelons of leadership in the church. The election of Mrs. Marjorie S. Matthews to the episcopacy by the North Central Jurisdictional Conference (1980) is testimony that the church is becoming more open to the future. In these signs of hope, let us rejoice. But in our rejoicing, let us remember that these are mere beginnings. It will require diligence, vigilance, and complete dedication to the community of Christ to assure continued progress in this direction. We may need to take a new look at some of our strategies, however well intentioned they may be. Take as an illustration the Ethnic Minority Local Church. The program of the General Conference to strengthen it, under the present circumstances and state of our society, is one that deserves great support. There are many already existing churches in communities where blacks predominantly reside that need to be strengthened, and there are communities where new churches should be established. But it would be wrong to conceive this as an end in itself. The same can be said of the churches organized on the basis of language, such as the Hispanic, Korean, and other groups. These churches are greatly needed as long as language is a barrier to communication and worship, and walls of isolation surround the people. It may be the best that can be done at the moment. There should be a major effort to educate young preachers in these churches for the professional ministry. At the same time, the church must seek ways to bring them all into a common fellowship, always looking to the time, and working toward it, when the church will be a community. It is still the desire of our Lord "that they may all be one." Lest we become complacent, let us remember that this is still his agenda.

In reviewing strategies it is not always necessary to set up study commissions and spend money and time studying something when the answers are already obvious. I have been a member of a number of study commissions during my life, and I am convinced that only a few of them made outstanding contributions to the solution of the problems. Some have done well, while some have thrown us into a greater quandary, and have done more to confuse the issue than to solve the problems. It is reminiscent of the man who said he stopped reading because reading confused him. Sometimes these study reports jumble the issues, when a little practical judgment could do the job. In many instances, it is not a new structure that the church needs, but a new spirit for which there is no substitute.

I sometimes feel that we anesthetize people with cliches instead of offering them renewal and hope through Christ. We arrange "priorities," and "lift up" issues; talk about "this point in time" and the "bottom line"; we ramble on with outworn terminology, and the multitudes sometimes turn us off. I shall always be grateful to a professor at New York University many years ago who gave me a low mark on an otherwise acceptable paper, because I used a number of cliches in it. I have been allergic to them ever since. They are not the best vehicle to convey the winds of the spirit.

Despite the many shortcomings of the church, I believe that its brightest days are still ahead, and in his own time God will bring it into full fruition.

It is interesting to stand at a pivotal point, view the landscape at a distance, and try to assess its meaning. I suppose much of it depends on the manner in which one sees life. In one sense, Langston Hughes testifies for many of us in his poem, *Mother to Son:*

> Well son, I'll tell you:
> Life for me ain't been no crystal stair . . .

But life has a deeper meaning, and for Belle and me it has also been an exhilarating story, as we have sought to participate in the moving drama of the last half century. What a privilege to have been identified with its pains, disciplined by its difficulties, inspired by its promises, and sustained by the conviction that "God was in Christ reconciling the world unto himself." We have been grateful for the opportunity to meet people in almost every land, people of different cultures, nationalities, religions, languages, political and economic systems, and varied horizons and world views. In so many instances they have been our teachers. There are only a few lessons one can learn that exceed those which are taught in the university of life. In a world of such prevalence of crime and violence, one is inclined to overlook the multitude of extraordinary people who reside in unexpected places. We have been the beneficiaries of the goodwill and moral support of a large number of these people.

The church has granted us the opportunity of participating in many institutions and movements which have done so much to shape our lives. We hope that in a small measure we have, along with many others, helped these institutions to do their work better.

We are grateful to the friends who have allowed us to share their sorrows and their joys, for in so doing, we have been illuminated by their faith, for the words of Paul come alive in them, ". . . suffering produces endurance, and endurance produces character, and character produces hope, and hope does not disappoint us."

A few weeks before my retirement in 1976 I tried to pull together what have been the guiding principles which have sustained me in whatever eventualities that emerge. Because they have been a source of strength to me I now share them with the reader:

1. God has not given up his dominion over the world.
2. Life without intrinsic values is built on a shaky foundation.
3. Positions and possessions are of relative value only.
4. What happens in you is far more important than what happens to you.
5. Life that is not nurtured by faith withers.
6. Mere adjustment to conditions and circumstances is a dangerous venture.
7. There are no simple problems nor simple solutions. In every problem there is a web of relationships which must be taken into consideration.
8. By the grace of God we are saved. None is so good as to earn it, none so bad as to be denied it.

These convictions have constantly surfaced and strengthened me during the life of my years.

Bibliography

Brawley, James P. *Two Centuries of Methodist Concern: Bondage, Freedom, and Education of Black People.* New York: Vantage Press, 1974.

Hughes, Langston. *Selected Poems.* New York: Alfred Knopf, 1959. Reprint. New York: Random House, 1974.

Marinelli, Lawrence A. *The New Liberia.* New York-London: Frederick A. Praeger Publishers, 1964.

Mathews, Basil J. *Booker T. Washington: Educator and Interracial Interpreter.* Cambridge, Mass.: Harvard University Press, 1948.

Swint, Henry L. *The Northern Teacher in the South, 1862-1870.* Nashville: Vanderbilt University Press, 1941. Reprint. New York: Random House, 1974.

top left: Bertha Ann Taylor, mother. *top right:* Prince A. Taylor, Sr., father. *center:* Prince A. Taylor, Jr. and wife Annie Bell enjoying a book together. *bottom:* Isabella Taylor, daughter.

top: President and Mrs. Tubman host dinner for the Taylors. Liberia, 1964. *center:* Drew University Day. Bishop Taylor welcomes new president, Dr. Paul Harden, 1975. *bottom:* Editor Taylor (left) interpreting to bishops the new format of the *Central Christian Advocate.*

top: President McCord, Rust College, confers honorary degree on Bishop Taylor. *center:* Bishop Corson congratulating Bishop Taylor upon presentation of St. George's Award Medal. Philadelphia. 1964. *bottom:* Bishop Taylor, newly elected chairman of the board of directors of Religion in American Life, receives the gavel from retiring chairman, Rev. Dr. Malvin H. Lundeen, Secretary of the Lutheran Church in America.

LIBERIA

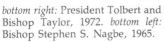

bottom right: President Tolbert and Bishop Taylor, 1972. *bottom left:* Bishop Stephen S. Nagbe, 1965.

top: President William V. S. Tubman, Liberia. *bottom:* The dedication of a home for girls at Gbarnga Methodist Mission. (*l. to r.*): a village chief; Rev. and Mrs. Gray, missionaries from Texas who founded the Mission; an instructor at the Mission; Bishop Taylor.

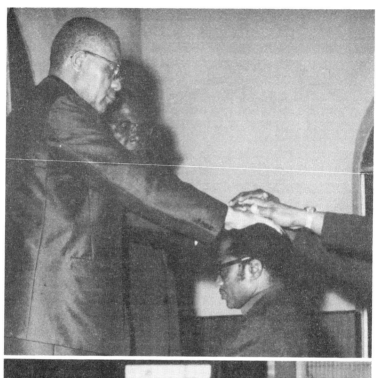

top left: The consecration of Bishop Bennie D. Warner after death of Stephen Nagbe, 1973. *bottom left:* Just after dedicating the Student Union Building at Cuttington College and Divinity School—an Episcopal college and divinity school. *top:* State dinner given in honor of Bishop Taylor by President and Mrs. Tubman. Executive Mansion, Monrovia, Liberia, 1965. *bottom:* Bishop Taylor installs Dr. Emilio Castro as first president of the newly organized Autonomous Methodist Church of Uraguay, 1969.

top: World Methodist Council Executive Committee meeting. Ghana, 1975. *center:* Central Pakistan Conference, 1968. *bottom:* Officers of the World Methodist Council. Tonga, 1972.